MURDER & MAYHEM

in Mendon and Honeoye Falls

- -

"Murderville" in Victorian New York

DIANE HAM AND LYNNE MENZ

THE
History
PRESS

Published by The History Press
Charleston, SC 29403
www.historypress.net

Copyright © 2013 by Diane Ham and Lynne Menz
All rights reserved

First published 2013

Manufactured in the United States

ISBN 978.1.62619.141.9

Library of Congress CIP data applied for.

Contents

Acknowledgements

No book ever writes itself. Without help from numerous individuals, this book would not have been possible. First and foremost, we thank Johanna O'Brien for planting the seed that grew into this book. We also thank Paul Worboys, Stan Worboys, Helen Stefano and Mike Roberts, who helped us as we gathered all the information. We thank Harry DeHollander and Emily Mansler, both retired from the Monroe County Sheriff's Office, for their help in "police matters." Special thanks go to our husbands, Rodney Ham, not only for his invaluable work on all our photos, and Wayne Menz, not only for his "tech" support every time the computer had a mind of its own, but also for their patience and understanding. Lastly, we thank Whitney Landis and everyone at The History Press for making this possible.

Introduction

T he Town of Mendon in upstate New York might be described as a quiet, somewhat well-to-do, semi-agricultural area. Today, the Village of Honeoye Falls within the town is what might be called a "bedroom" community. It is a quiet little village where many people even today lock their doors only at night. That was not always the case.

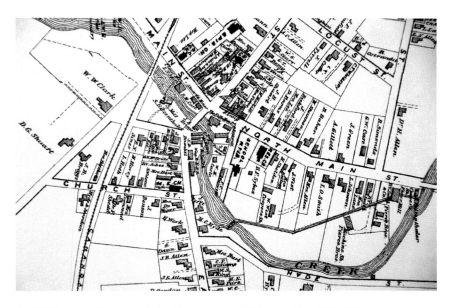

An 1872 map of Honeoye Falls. *From the* Atlas of Monroe Co., NY, *1872.*

In years past, the village was the center of commerce for the town, with prosperous mills, manufacturing, retail shops and two railroad lines—the New York Central and the Lehigh Valley—that connected it to the rest of the United States and the world. In the mid-1800s, this quiet little village was anything but quiet. Horse stealing was commonplace, with white horses turning black overnight. Saloons and taverns were numerous. Street fights and barroom brawls were common, especially on Saturday nights after the immigrant workers on the railroads and water conduit were paid. Drunks were confined to the village jail, known as the "lockup," which was located in the village hall. It was at this time that the quiet Village of Honeoye Falls earned the name "Murderville."

It was this nickname of Murderville that sparked our interest. It was briefly mentioned by former historians of the village and longtime residents. One such resident, Paul Worboys, even constructed a time line of events that were related to the ominous moniker, but few particulars were ever given—until now. We have waded through census records, old newspapers and various other sources, and little by little we have filled in the particulars. It was hard to believe that these murders actually took place in our own backyards.

We hope you find these events as interesting as we did.

1

Honeoye Falls' Good Name Tainted

William Barrows and Edward Lake, August 11, 1899

After the years following the Revolutionary War, the building of the Erie Canal and the coming of railroads to West Mendon (now Honeoye Falls) and the Town of Mendon, New York, social and economic attitudes began to change. Many Europeans who had settled in the New England states, eastern New York, Pennsylvania and New Jersey were being crowded out and desired to own more land. Many of them came to western New York, including to the Town of Mendon and the Village of Honeoye Falls. Many folks purchased land, and others roamed around, filling their days with opportunity or more undesirable activities.

One young Honeoye Falls lad of fourteen was the first to have his name written in the Admittance Book at the Western House of Refuge, which was opened for delinquents in 1849 in Rochester, New York. According to a Rochester newspaper of August 11, 1849, William Barrows was committed for burglarizing a house and for associating with idle and vicious boys. The records of the Western House of Refuge indicated that William Barrows was "pretty and intelligent but seemed to have been considerable of a rogue." Thirty-eight boys were admitted that first year.

William Barrows was born in the Town of Rush, Monroe County, to American parents who had moved to West Mendon. His parents were temperate. His father, Jarvis Barrows, was a tailor and owned his house and lot in Mendon.

William had attended school pretty regularly until the previous two years. The summer before he was admitted to the "House," William worked

Western House of Refuge, Rochester, New York, built in 1849. *Reprint courtesy of Rochester Historical Society.*

on a farm. He said that for the past three years he had been in the habit of associating with idle and vicious boys and frequently committed theft. Once he broke into a grocery store. The offense for which he was sent to the institution was breaking into a private home in company with Edward Lake and stealing eighteen dollars. This had occurred the previous winter, at which time the boys were arrested and "admitted to bail" from time to time until they were sent to the House of Refuge. In April 1852, William Barrows was discharged to the care of his father, who was planning to move to the West in an attempt to save his "recreant" son.

Edward Lake, age thirteen, was also committed to the Western House of Refuge on August 11, 1849. He was born to American parents in Monroe County. His father, Robert A. Lake, was a farmer and lived in West Mendon as well. He had recently sold his farm and was planning to move to Wisconsin. Edward always lived at home, went to school and worked on the farm.

When he was admitted, Edward said he had never associated with bad boys or committed any criminal offenses until the previous fall, when he fell in company with William Barrows, with whom he committed two or three petty offenses and finally broke into a private home when the family was absent, stole eighteen dollars and was soon after arrested. He was also "admitted to bail" until the next term of the court, when they were both sent to the House. He read fairly well but often referred to himself as stupid. He did not appear to be vicious.

On March 6, 1850, Edward was discharged to his parents, who were about to move to Wisconsin. He had been in the House seven months and on the whole had conducted himself well. His parents were respectable and owned some property.

On April 19, 1854, Edward visited the House of Refuge. He had grown so large that it was difficult to recognize him. He was living with his father near Troy, Walworth County, Wisconsin. He said they owned a farm of 150 acres of land valued at between $40 to $100 per acre with good buildings and stock valued at $2,000. Edward seemed to be a respectable young man.

It is hoped that these two young men learned their lessons that stealing and other forms of crime were not acceptable and that they found ways to become good, respectable citizens. It is not known what became of either of them.

2

"I'm a Dead Man"

The Murder of Constable Starr, October 30, 1857

The Lockes, William and Lovisa, settled in the Village of Honeoye Falls in the 1830s. Their son, Manley, was born on February 22, 1836. He grew into a headstrong, often violent young man. According to his mother, he showed no interest in learning and was always prone to violence. The *Rochester Union and Advertiser*, in an article on November 7, 1857, indicated that "Manley Locke is a desperate character and has been the terror of the Village for a long time. When under the influence of alcohol, he was extremely desperate."

His first encounter with village constable Benjamin Starr occurred on July 3, 1857. On that day, Manley had been drinking and was most likely drunk and in a state of what witnesses would describe as depression. He went to his parents' home and, arming himself with a table knife from a drawer, confronted his mother. "He was crying and had a wild look in his eyes," said his mother, recounting the event. She asked him, "Manley, you would not hurt me, your mother, would you?" He did not reply. When his father entered the room, Manley moved toward him. His father recounted, "He looked like a creature that was scared. He came toward me and said he must kill me." At this point, William Locke left the house, and Manley followed him outside. He repeated again that he must kill his father, all the while crying. When Manley reentered the house, Mr. Locke asked a neighbor, Mr. Valentine, to see if he could get the knife away from him. According to Mr. Locke, Valentine went into the house, and after Valentine spoke with Manley for a while, Manley laid down his knife. Manley gave

New York Central Depot in Honeoye Falls, taken circa 1900. *Courtesy of Honeoye Falls/ Mendon Historical Society.*

no reason for feeling that he must kill his father. After awhile, Manley left the house and went to the depot across the street, where he was seen walking around the platform.

After Manley left, Mrs. Locke went into the village to see the magistrate, Mr. Cummings, and apparently recounted what took place at the house. Mr. Cummings sent Constable Starr to arrest Manley. Starr found Manley at the depot, arrested him and, after fining him ten dollars, took him home in irons and released him after his father paid the fine. It was later claimed, at Manley Locke's murder trial, that upon his release by Starr, Manley had said, "If Starr ever attempts to arrest me again, another star will shine."

On Friday afternoon, October 30, 1857, Manley Locke and two companions, one named Badger and the other Spellacy, were in Mr. Peachee's tavern. Locke started a quarrel with an Englishman who was minding his own business. Locke asked the man if he could fight, and when the man answered, "No," Locke knocked the man down at the door and chased him down the street, beating and kicking him.

The injured man complained to the magistrate, Mr. Cummings, who issued another warrant for Manley Locke's arrest. Constable Starr was again sent to arrest Locke.

When Manley Locke heard that Constable Starr had a warrant for his arrest, he repeated his threat: "He will never arrest another man if he arrests me." Locke was armed with a shoe knife with a sharp point and a set of "leaden knuckles." Witnesses had seen him sharpening the knife two days before the murder.

At about 7:00 p.m., Constable Starr arrived at the tavern to arrest Manley Locke. The tavern was full. Constable Starr knew that Locke had a knife. Witnesses testified that Locke had "high words" with Constable Starr. When Starr grabbed Locke to arrest him, Locke struck Starr in the face with the leaden knuckles, breaking his nose. Locke started to run out the door. Starr pursued him and caught him, all the while calling for help. Locke then stabbed Starr twice. The first attack was through his arm, and the second entered the aorta, inflicting a half-inch-long wound, according to Dr. Avery, who examined the wound. Starr fell into the arms of one of the onlookers at the tavern and gasped, "I am a dead man." He expired within three minutes.

Meanwhile, Locke and his two companions, Badger and Spellacy, ran about a mile and hid in a cornfield behind a shock of corn. Their pursuers drove them from their hiding place. Locke was finally caught as he was climbing a fence to escape. His pursuers grabbed him and threw him to the ground with such force as to cause him to release the knife. Locke was such a powerful man that it took the strength of three men to subdue him. Locke confessed to the party who arrested him that he had, in fact, stabbed Constable Starr.

The coroner's inquest found that Constable Starr's death was the result of his stab wounds. Manley Locke was held for trial and charged with murder.

Constable Starr was buried in Honeoye Falls Cemetery. His obituary in the *Rochester Union and Advertiser* on November 7, 1857, read:

> *Mr. Starr was an esteemed citizen of Mendon and was about fifty-six years of age. He leaves a wife and several children, most of who [sic] have arrived at majority. His family is in deep distress and has the sympathy of their neighbors and fellow citizens, who are deeply indignant at the act. They hope they are relieved forever from the presence of the wicked perpetrator of the deed. Mr. Starr was a brother of the gentleman by that name who is Postmaster at Medina, Orleans County. His funeral took place yesterday* [November 6] *and was largely attended.*

The trial of Manley Locke began in October 1858 and "excited great interest," not only for the facts, but also for Locke's unusual defense. The facts of the case were indisputable. The murder was committed in the sight of many

Left: Benjamin Starr's gravestone, Honeoye Falls Cemetery. *Author's collection.*

Below: Auburn Prison, Auburn, New York. *Courtesy of Rochester Public Library.*

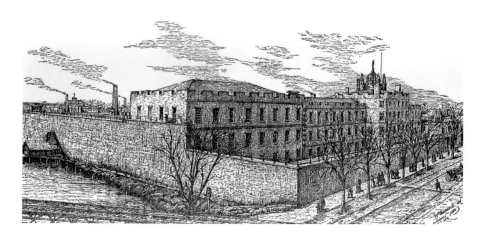

witnesses. Manley Locke murdered Constable Starr. The real issue of the case concerned premeditation. The question concerned Locke's "mental state." Locke was known as a violent man. He had threatened to hurt his mother and kill his father. He was known as the "terror of the village." Yet at his trial, he was fully supported by his family, who testified that he suffered from mental illness. Family members from Michigan, Ohio, Pennsylvania, Kentucky and Virginia—all persons of reputable standing—attended and supported him at his trial. The defense argued that Locke was "never a master of his actions: that at school he evinced no capacity for knowledge and that both his mother and father were in fear for their lives from him." Some of the witnesses for the defense testified to indications of insanity in the Locke family going back three generations. It was a hard-fought trial, and Locke was well represented.

It took the jury about a day to reach a verdict. When the verdict was read, Locke was convicted, but not on the charge of murder. Instead, the jury found him guilty of manslaughter. Locke was remanded to Monroe County Jail (also known as the Blue Eagle Jail) in Rochester to await his sentencing.

The case then took an unanticipated turn. On December 13, 1858, Locke and fourteen other prisoners escaped from the jail. Using watch springs, they sawed through the iron bars in five places, making an opening ten by sixteen inches through which they could crawl. To lower themselves to the river below the jail, they took the halter with which Ira Stout had been executed some years before. It is supposed that they chose the night of December 13 because Mr. Gatens, one of the night watchmen, had gone to the country to see his family, thereby leaving the night force at the jail reduced. The escape probably took place about midnight after bed check and was not discovered until the next morning, giving the escapees, Manley Locke among them, about an eight-hour head start.

According to the *Rochester Union and Advertiser*, on December 15 Sheriff Babcock received a telegram from N. Dennison of Mount Morris notifying him of the capture of Manley Locke. Locke was returned to Rochester. On December 26 and again on December 30, Locke tried to escape. Both attempts were unsuccessful.

On January 4, 1859, Manley Locke received his sentence under the conviction of manslaughter in the first degree. He was attended by his sister, one of his uncles and J.H. Martindale, Esq., his counsel. The district attorney admitted that if the case was not murder, it was manslaughter in the third degree. He went on to say that Locke was of weak mind and appealed to the court on behalf of Locke's relatives, who "were worthy of pity and would suffer most by the infliction of a severe sentence." After discussion among the

Gravestone of Manley T. Locke, Honeoye Falls Cemetery. *Author's collection.*

members of the court and a consulting of the statutes, the prisoner, Manley Locke, was brought forward. Locke swore that he was an American by birth, twenty-two years of age, could read and write, had no trade and had religious instruction as an Episcopalian. Judge Strong asked Locke if he had anything to say after hearing the charges and the verdict, and Locke made no reply. The court then sentenced Manley Locke to life in Auburn Prison. Following the sentencing, District Attorney Hudson moved that Manley Locke be sent to Auburn Prison "forthwith" because of his three attempts to escape.

There is one more twist to the case of Manley Locke. In 1865, for reasons unknown, Locke was pardoned and released from Auburn Prison. In 1866, he married Caroline Dean. They had a daughter in 1867 and a son, Maynard Locke, in 1869. His wife, Caroline, died in March 1872. Sometime between 1869 and 1879, Manley Locke was once again sent to prison, this time to the Buffalo Penitentiary, where on October 20, 1879, he died of "progressive dissipation." He was buried back in Honeoye Falls, where a simple stone reading, "M.T. Locke 1836–1879," marks his grave in the Honeoye Falls Cemetery. He was only forty-three years old.

3

Insanity Kills Again

The Murder of Margaret DuPlante, May 31, 1858

On May 31, 1858, the second murder in less than a year was committed in Honeoye Falls. Yacente DuPlante was arrested for killing his wife, Margaret, for some unknown reason.

The DuPlante family consisted of Yacente; his wife, Margaret; and their six children—Albert, sixteen; Rachel, fourteen; Sarah, ten; Margaret, nine; Francis L., six; and a three-month-old infant. Mr. DuPlante was a cooper by trade, and he and his family lived with Asa Gillette in a stone house in Honeoye Falls (at least at the time of the 1855 census). Mr. Gillette was also a cooper, so DuPlante was probably learning the cooper's trade from him. DuPlante had been working for Hiram Finch until three or four weeks before the incident. They were very poor. He indicated that he had quit his job because of poor health so was not working at the time.

On that fateful day, the family had eaten breakfast, and Mrs. DuPlante asked her husband to go and get her some flour since the flour bin was empty. He went to the store of Ogden & Case to get the flour. While he was there, he asked Mr. Case to loan him a gun and load it since he had no powder or shot. He claimed he was going to shoot chickens. It was an ordinary single-barreled shotgun.

DuPlante arrived back home about 8:30 a.m. with the gun. He put the gun in one corner of the room, where his wife and children were, put away the flour and sat down. Mrs. DuPlante was bathing the baby. She asked her husband why he didn't go to work, as she didn't see how they were going stay alive. He replied that he was weak and unable to work. He thought

Asa Gillette's cut-stone house, Honeoye Falls, New York, built circa 1825; this is where the DuPlante family also lived. *Courtesy of Honeoye Falls/Mendon Historical Society.*

they should move to the city. His wife objected and said that he could go ahead and move, but she would not go with him. After Mrs. DuPlante put the baby in the cradle, she went to the pantry, passing the chair where her husband was sitting. After a short time, DuPlante got up and took the gun from the corner, placed the muzzle a few inches from his wife's right side and discharged it. The whole charge entered her body near her waist. Margaret DuPlante turned part way around, screamed and immediately fell to the floor. She probably expired within six or eight minutes.

DuPlante then told his oldest daughter to take care of the baby, who was screaming violently, and went out into the street intending to give himself up. His six-year-old son was with him. The young boy was crying, "Oh dear, oh dear!" and attracted the attention of Judge C.C. Davidson, Esq. When questioned, the child told him that his father had shot his mother. Mr. Davidson took the gun from DuPlante and returned with him to the house. DuPlante was then arrested, taken before a magistrate and fully committed for murder. Deputy Sheriff Yorks took him to the Monroe County Jail in Rochester at about noon. DuPlante made no attempt to escape.

Coroner Quinn was summoned to the scene of the murder. The following men were impaneled as a jury of inquest: A.D.J. McDonald, foreman; E.P. Lacy; S. Rand; Asa Pride; C.T. Whitney; Albe Allen; Stephen Barrett; Sylvester Kellogg; James Annis; Thomas Hill; Richard Ostrander; and Adam W. Willis.

Drs. Bly, of Rochester, and B.H. Benham of Honeoye Falls made a postmortem examination. They found a gunshot wound in Margaret DuPlante's right side, severing a rib near the spine, wounding the lower portion of the right lung and a portion of the liver and then entering the spine. The shots were imbedded in the spine, some of which they removed.

After hearing the testimony in the case, the jury found that Margaret R. DuPlante, the deceased, "came to her death by a gun-shot wound, from a gun in the hands of and discharged by Yacente DuPlante, her husband, on the 31st day of May, 1858, at Honeoye Falls, in the county of Monroe." Testimony was made that DuPlante had talked a great deal about being made "King over all" and sometimes spoke of his youngest child as "Christ," while at other times he would call him "Anti-Christ." During the time he wasn't working, he claimed that there was no necessity for him to work on account of his royal position and said that he was not going to earn his bread twice. He had sold all his tools. Mrs. DuPlante was quite upset with him for refusing to work, and there seemed to be problems between them because of it. DuPlante had told several people recently that he was thinking about getting rid of his wife. He talked about a divorce and thought about finding five or six young girls for wives when Mrs. DuPlante was disposed of.

The inquest was concluded at about 12:30 p.m., and Coroner Quinn immediately made a commitment. DuPlante was taken to Monroe County Jail and held prisoner. The children were taken to the Rochester Orphan Asylum on Hubbell Park. Margaret DuPlante was buried in the Honeoye Falls Cemetery.

Gravestone of Margaret DuPlante, Honeoye Falls Cemetery, erected 2008. *Author's collection.*

Monroe County Insane Asylum, Rochester, New York. *Courtesy of C.W. Woodward.*

Yacente DuPlante was a man about medium height and of fair proportions. He had a long face and sallow complexion. He appeared to be rather intelligent but was not educated. He spoke fair English. He said he didn't know what made him commit the dreadful deed. He did show some emotion. He stated that the previous summer he had a feeling of weakness in his chest that sometimes made him feel irritable and out of patience with people. He said he never quarreled much with his wife.

However, according to the *Geneva Gazette* of June 9, 1858, "For several weeks before the deed was committed, his mind had been unsettled on religious matters, and Mrs. DuPlante had said several times that she feared he would kill her."

According to the *Rochester Union and Advertiser* for December 13, 1858, there was a jailbreak at the Monroe County Jail, but Yacente DuPlante refused to leave with Manley Locke and others who did escape that night. DuPlante tipped off officers about this incident.

Late in 1859, DuPlante was found not guilty by reason of insanity at his trial. He was taken to the Utica Insane Asylum.

On April 25, 1861, Albert DuPlante, son of Yacente DuPlante, enlisted in the Civil War for three months in Downey's Thirteenth New York Volunteers. This period was extended to two years. He fought at Antietam and Fredericksburg.

On December 26, 1866, Yacente Duplante was discharged from the Utica Insane Asylum and taken to the Monroe County Insane Asylum. This transfer caused less of a strain on Utica's expenses. The Monroe County records indicated that "Jasinthe Duplante" was released from the Monroe County Insane Asylum on February 11, 1867. His condition was "Well." It is not known at this time what happened to him, when he died or where he was buried.

4

Burglary of the Post Office

January 20, 1859

Every small town, or in this case, village, has its infamous characters from time to time, and Andrew Spellacy seemed to be one of those in Honeoye Falls. In the twenty short years of his life, he managed to make quite a name for himself in the village, a name that usually meant trouble. In 1857, he was an accomplice of Manley Locke when he killed Constable Benjamin Starr, and although indicted as an accessory, he was never brought to trial. Now in 1859, he was by his own admission involved in the burglary of both the Honeoye Falls Post Office and the A.C. Allen Drugstore.

The Honeoye Falls Post Office was located in a harness shop at that time. G.B. McBride was the postmaster. On Saturday, January 19, 1859, he was working late. He left the office at about nine o'clock. Sometime after that and before he returned on Sunday evening, burglars entered the post office. They pried open a back shutter, climbed through a window and then broke through a door in the partition between the harness shop and the post office. In the post office, they took stamps and some cash before they departed by the same way they had come. On Sunday evening, when McBride returned to the post office, he found the work of the "rogues." He reported that they had taken about thirty dollars' worth of stamps and another twenty dollars in cash from one of the forty or fifty letters torn open and left scattered about the floor.

When word of the burglary got out on Monday morning, villagers rushed to the post office to see what had been done. Among those was Andrew Williams. Williams, a lad of only nineteen years, already had an unsavory reputation and was thought to be "of the bad class." When Postmaster McBride saw Williams there, he thought that he might have been involved and was there to "spy" on what was being done about the theft.

In order to catch the thieves, a plan was put into action. The newspaper was asked to delay publication of the burglary. It was thought that if nothing were printed about the burglary, maybe the "rogues" would contact the Rochester Police, county sheriff or even the United States Marshal and offer the stolen stamps for sale. Unfortunately, that did not happen. So, suspecting that Williams and maybe Spellacy were involved, a trap was set. Spellacy and, soon after, Williams were caught, and some of the stolen stamps were recovered. Spellacy and Williams were taken to Rochester for examination before the United States commissioner.

In the murder of Benjamin Starr by Manley Locke, Spellacy had been named as an accomplice, but by turning on Locke and testifying against him, he was allowed to go free. Apparently, he thought this same strategy might work again. As it happened, not long before the post office was burglarized, A.C. Allen Drugstore was also burglarized, and twenty-five dollars in cash was taken. Allen purchased a new safe, and shortly after it was installed, the store was burglarized again and the new safe was broken open. Spellacy admitted that he had been involved in these two incidents and named another, William Lord, as the mastermind of the operations.

Lord was a man with a questionable reputation. He supposedly made his home in the northern part of the Town of Mendon. He was by occupation a traveling clock repairer and tinker. He was arrested, and with Spellacy's testimony, he was charged with the Allen Drugstore burglary. This time, however, Spellacy was not let off.

On May 24, 1859, Andrew Spellacy pleaded guilty to the indictment of robbing the Honeoye Falls Post Office. He was sentenced to four years in Auburn State Prison. Andrew Williams, Spellacy's accomplice, also pleaded guilty and because of his age was sentenced to five years in the Western House of Refuge. This last sentence was the first of its kind, as Williams was sentenced to a fixed amount of time, and it was considered a questionable sentence since it was not in accordance with New York State law regulating Houses of Refuge.

There is no information about what happened to Andrew Williams from this point on. Andrew Spellacy, however, served his term or at least part of it as he is listed in the 1860 census as a "convict" with his parents in Mendon. In February 1863, he enlisted in the Civil War. Civil War records state that he enlisted in Rochester at the age of twenty-three in the Fourth Heavy

Artillery Regiment. He died on February 2, 1864, of disease at Fort Ethan Allen, Virginia, and was buried at Soldiers Home National Cemetery in Washington, D.C.

As for the Village of Honeoye Falls, after the arrest and conviction of Spellacy and Williams, there were fewer "rogues" on its streets.

5

Another Starr Murdered

Murder of John Wesley Starr, July 21, 1863

T he Civil War began with the firing on Fort Sumter by the Confederates in 1861. Initially, Northern men rushed to enlist, but by 1862, many of these initial enlistments were up. With the North having suffered numerous bloody defeats, enlistments took a sharp decline while the need for soldiers increased. President Lincoln requested that Congress pass a draft law, but the law had a loophole. Drafted men who did not want to serve could hire a substitute or proxy to enlist for them. It was not uncommon for a man to enlist as a proxy, later desert from the army and then enlist as a proxy for someone else.

In 1862, John "Wesley" Starr was drafted into the Union army. He did not want to serve, so he hired James Murphy as his proxy. Murphy enlisted as Starr's proxy in Captain William Downey's Company K of the Thirteenth Infantry in August 1862. Apparently, army life did not suit Murphy because in November 1862, at Harpers Ferry, he deserted and later returned to the Honeoye Falls area claiming that it was all Starr's fault because Starr had induced him to enlist. Several months later, in July 1863, James Murphy killed John Wesley Starr.

John Wesley Starr, age twenty-nine, was the son of Benjamin Starr, the former constable of Honeoye Falls who had been murdered in 1857. Wesley Starr was employed as a bartender in the tavern of the Wilcox House, a prominent hotel on Main Street in Honeoye Falls. According to Starr, on Tuesday afternoon, July 21, 1863, at about 3:00 p.m., Murphy took a glass of beer at the Wilcox tavern, where Starr worked. Murphy then left and

West Main Street, Honeoye Falls, looking at the Wilcox House Hotel (center) circa 1907. *Courtesy of Honeoye Falls/Mendon Historical Society.*

Wilcox House Hotel, Honeoye Falls, New York, circa 1861. *Courtesy of Honeoye Falls/Mendon Historical Society and Geoff Tesch.*

returned again between 8:00 and 9:00 p.m., asking for something to drink. At first, Starr told him that he had sold out, but finally he simply told him that he could have no more liquor. Murphy replied, "You can go to h--l." Starr responded, "So can you." At that point, Starr left the tavern. At about 11:00 p.m., Murphy returned to the tavern, this time wanting a room. Starr told him that the beds were full, but if Murphy went to Ward's (the other tavern in town), he (Starr) would pay for his lodging. Since Murphy didn't know where Ward's was, Starr agreed to show him. Both Murphy and Starr left the tavern, going about "two or three rods," and Starr pointed out Ward's place to Murphy. At that point, Murphy said that he would not go to that tavern and insisted on returning to the Wilcox House. Starr said, "No," whereupon Murphy pulled out a knife and stabbed Starr in the side. Starr ran into the Wilcox House, bolted the door and called Dr. Benham, who boarded there, and told him that he had been wounded.

When Dr. Benham came down to the tavern, he found Starr had fainted. When Starr regained consciousness, he related what had happened to Dr. Benham, who called the village constable. By the next day, July 22, a second doctor, Dr. Moore, had seen Starr. His examination of Starr found that the knife had entered the spleen, thereby inflicting a fatal wound. Dr. Moore stated that Starr was dying. He died later that day.

John Wesley Starr was laid to rest in the family plot in the Honeoye Falls Cemetery; however, his gravestone is now missing. He rests near his father, Benjamin Starr, who was also murdered in 1858. Both father and son were victims of what amounts to senseless killings.

After stabbing Starr, James Murphy left the village and traveled east. When he came to a farmhouse, he crawled through a window of the house and fell asleep. The family who lived in the house heard him and drove him out. At four o'clock in the morning, he finally reached his home in Mendon, about five miles east of the Village of Honeoye Falls. There, he was arrested by Constable McWilliams, who had been notified by Dr. Benham.

Justice of the Peace L.N. Allen, at Starr's request, had issued a warrant for Murphy's arrest. On July 22, after he was arrested, Murphy was brought before Justice Allen and examined in the room where Starr lay dying. Murphy was represented during that examination by legal counsel. At that time, Starr recounted the events of the previous day and night. This dying disposition of Starr would later be used in Murphy's trial. Following this, Murphy was taken to the jail in the city of Rochester to await trial. Murphy claimed to know nothing of the affair, as he must have committed the act while drunk. He also said he never had any intention of harming Starr.

The inquest was held on July 23 by Coroner Treat. The postmortem conducted by Drs. Benham, Allen and Miner concluded that the knife had punctured Starr's small intestine, resulting in inflammation of the intestines and eventually death. Testimony at the inquest suggested that there was no provocation for the assault. There was no evidence that Murphy harbored any unkind feelings toward Starr up to the time he inflicted the fatal wound. It was noted that Murphy was drunk at the time, and when under the influence of liquor, Murphy had a propensity for using a knife. After listening to all the testimony, the inquest jury concluded that Starr died from the wound inflicted by James Murphy with an instrument unknown to the jury.

On October 14, 1863, James Murphy was arraigned in the Court of Oyer and Terminer. He was indicted for the murder of John W. Starr. He pleaded not guilty and demanded trial. M.S. Newton, Esq., appeared as his counsel. His trial date was set for January 1864.

The trial of James Murphy began on Monday, February 8, 1864. Judge Welles presided with Justices Swayne and Wright as associates. The prosecution case was conducted by District Attorney Bowman, assisted by George W. Miller, Esq., city attorney; Messrs. Newton and Ripson and J.D. Husbands, Esq., appeared for the defendant. Murphy was charged with murder.

The counsel for the defendant proposed on behalf of Murphy that he put in a plea of guilty of manslaughter and take the sentence that the court might impose, as there was no doubt that Murphy had, in fact, stabbed Starr. However, after some argument, the court refused the proposition, and the trial commenced.

The *Union and Advertiser*, a local Rochester newspaper, noted that the attendance of spectators in the court was not large and that many witnesses had been called by both the defense and prosecution. It also commented that there did not appear to be much cause for Murphy to have stabbed Starr. "Murphy was simply drunk, and whiskey did the mischief." In the paper's opinion, that was pretty much all there was to the case. It did note that Wesley Starr was the son of Benjamin Starr, who was killed in the same village some years before by Manley Locke, who was at this time in state prison convicted of manslaughter. It went on to say that "if the killing of the elder Starr was manslaughter, it will be very difficult to make a case of murder out of the killing of his son. But courts and juries are very erratic."

Mr. Miller opened the case for the people. The prosecution argued that there was more to Murphy's actions than merely a drunk man wielding a knife. It not only called witnesses to testify about the events of that fateful night in the Wilcox Hotel but also called witnesses to testify that Murphy threatened revenge on Starr as a result of his enlisting as Starr's proxy in Captain Downey's Company K, Thirteenth Regiment. George Richardson, who belonged to the same regiment as Murphy, testified that he had heard Murphy say that Starr had induced him to enlist, that Starr was a mean fellow and that he wished Starr was dead.

The prosecution also called Drs. Benham and Miner, as well as Justice Allen and Mr. Davidson, to testify about the statements that Starr made as he lay dying. Justice Allen was the magistrate before whom Starr was examined, and Mr. Davidson took his testimony on that examination. The prosecution also proposed that Mr. Starr's testimony, given by him after he was advised that he would not recover, be accepted by the court. The defense objected to this last testimony, and after an argument of considerable length, the court accepted the testimony.

There was little that the defense could do to defend Murphy. It concluded that he had, in fact, stabbed Starr but argued that Murphy was "crazy under the influence of liquor" and did so without any malice or premeditation. It called on John W. Murphy, son of the defendant, as its first witness. He testified that "when under the influence of liquor, his father acted strangely and was apparently unconscious of what he did." Several other witnesses also concurred that, when drunk, Murphy acted like "a crazy man and did not know what he did."

Richard Ward, the owner of the hotel and tavern a short distance down the street from the Wilcox Hotel, testified that Murphy had been in his establishment the afternoon of the murder. He had been drinking there for part of the afternoon and was "very drunk."

In an attempt to counter the testimony given by George Richardson regarding Murphy's "wishing Starr was dead," the defense called Warren Cummins and others. They testified that Murphy frequently told them before he enlisted for Starr that he would like to enlist.

The defense concluded its case on February 11, the third day of the trial. The prosecution used the rest of that day to call witnesses to testify that Murphy was only slightly intoxicated on the fateful day. They testified that Murphy had been intoxicated in the afternoon but then had the appearance of being only slightly so by that evening.

On Friday, February 13, Mr. Husbands summed up the case on behalf of the defense. He admitted to the killing of Starr by Murphy but argued that, at the time, Murphy was of unsound mind due to the influence of alcohol. He also concluded that there was no conclusive evidence to show that Murphy had committed the murder with any malice against Starr. As there was no

Entrance to Auburn Prison, Auburn, New York. Photo by Rich Bellamy.

premeditation, Murphy should only be found guilty of manslaughter in the third degree and not murder. Mr. Husband's summation took three hours.

Mr. Bowman summed up the case for the prosecution. The prosecution argued that Murphy had often been heard to say he wished Starr was dead and that he had threatened to take revenge for inducing him to enlist in the Thirteenth Regiment. He also maintained that Murphy was not drunk at the time of the stabbing and that he knew exactly what he was doing.

The case went to the jury on Monday morning, July 15, at ten o'clock. The jury deliberated and returned with its verdict in only two hours. It found James Murphy guilty of murder in the second degree. Murphy showed emotion at the pronouncement of the verdict.

On the day of his sentencing, the judge asked Murphy if he had anything to say. Murphy replied that he did not. Before passing sentence, Judge Welles briefly went over the history of the case. He alluded to Murphy's "indulgence in the use of intoxicating liquors as the cause of his trouble." He approved the finding of the jury and fixed the sentence at the lowest he could under the statute—ten years and three months in Auburn State Prison. Due to Murphy's age, which was estimated to be between fifty-six and sixty, it is thought that he would not survive the sentence in state prison.

James Murphy did not survive the sentence. He died in Auburn Prison on October 9, 1870.

6

Murder or Self-Defense?

The Murder of William Gates, November 8, 1869

On November 18, 1869, William Gates of Honeoye Falls, New York, died of head wounds received during an altercation with John and Catherine Donlon in the Donlon home in the Village of Honeoye Falls. That is an indisputable fact. It is also a fact that the wounds came from blows delivered by John and his wife, Catherine. It appears to be a clear-cut case of murder, but nothing is ever really clear. Prejudice, hard feelings and revenge all play a part.

William Gates lived in Honeoye Falls. He was a laborer in charge of the track hands for the New York Central Railroad. He was married, and in fact his in-laws, Richard and Jeanette Barnum, lived in half of a duplex; the Donlon family occupied the other half. Donlon had worked for Gates on the railroad. Gates had, in fact, fired Donlon shortly before his death, and there was animosity between the two. Gates had been overheard to say several times, "If that damned Irishman [Donlon] doesn't keep out of my way, I will fix him." He was overheard on at least one occasion saying that to Donlon.

As stated before, John Donlon and his family lived in half of a duplex on Main Street in Honeoye Falls. At the time of the Gates killing, Donlon might have been unemployed, having been fired by Gates. He, too, had been overheard saying on at least one occasion, "There goes that damned long-legged Bill Gates; I ought to have his heart's blood, for he says he will have mine."

It was clear long before the murder of Gates that both he and Donlon disliked each other. Each had made threats against the other—violent threats that were heard and witnessed by several village residents. So it was possible that given the opportunity, either man could have murdered the other if an opportunity arose.

Just after dusk on November 8, the Barnums, Gates's in-laws, and the Donlons were at home in the house they shared, with a common central entrance with a door to each side and a common wall between. Each residence had a back door, and both families shared the barn in the back. It was a quiet evening. What happened next depends on who is recounting the events.

According to Mrs. Jeanette Barnum, her son-in-law, William Gates, stopped by. A few minutes later, her husband left. She, along with her daughter Cynthia and Gates, was in the residence, and they heard "remarks" about Mrs. Gates coming either through the wall that divided the two residences or from a door in the wall. Upon hearing the remarks, Gates left the Barnum side of the house and knocked on the door to the Donlon side of the house.

When Donlon opened the door, Gates asked Donlon what the talk he had overheard was about. According to Mrs. Barnum, Donlon replied that it was none of his business, and then Gates said, "Why, then, do you call my wife such names?" Donlon denied it and jerked Gates inside the house and onto the floor, where he began beating him in the face with his fists. Mrs. Donlon picked up something flat from the stove. It was thought to have been a skillet, though it was never actually identified as such, and began striking Gates in the face about four or five times. Donlon held Gates's hands away from his face so that Mrs. Donlon could hit him. While hitting him, Mrs. Donlon swore that she would kill him. Mrs. Barnum said she heard Donlon tell his wife to kill him, and she saw Mrs. Donlon pick up an instrument "with a handle like a knife" and stab Gates in the face. At this point, Mr. Barnum arrived. Seeing Gates on the floor, he told Donlon that he had killed Gates and to stop. Donlon got off Gates, and Mr. Barnum pulled Gates by the heels out of the house and onto the front step. Mrs. Donlon, according to Mrs. Barnum, said that she was glad they had killed him and, following Gates, continued to strike him until he was finally pulled out the door. Barnum sat Gates, who neither spoke nor moved, against a door in the latticework of the house and went to get the doctor. "After about five minutes," said Mrs. Barnum, "Gates got up and went down the street." Mrs. Barnum later testified that Gates had made no effort to strike Donlon.

Mrs. Barnum's account of the events was backed up by her daughter Cynthia, who was at home. She heard some of the conversation through the wall but did not understand it. She followed her mother to the Donlons' door and witnessed Mrs. Donlon striking Gates but was unable to identify the object Mrs. Donlon used. She also testified that Donlon held Gates's hands so he could not protect himself from the blows, but she did not hear Donlon or his wife say anything. "I ran to the front door and saw a man coming along. I raised the cry of murder and asked the man to help," she said, "but he said he didn't want to make a fuss."

There is, of course, Richard Barnum's account of the events. He was not present at the beginning, but he did pull Gates from the house. Barnum was Gates's father-in-law. He was also employed as a carter for the railroad. He claimed that he had often heard Donlon threaten to take revenge on Gates for having fired him. He had been in the barn with Donlon prior to Gates's arrival at the house. He was not at home when the whole affair between Gates and Donlon began, and as he arrived home, he claimed he heard a shout of "Murder!" It was at that moment that he ran into Donlon's half of the house and saw Gates lying on the floor in the doorway. "I saw Donlon with his left knee on his [Gates's] heart hitting him with his fist and Mrs. Donlon hitting him on the head with some iron thing." He then pulled Gates out of the house onto the step and sat him up with help from a passerby. He said he saw Gates later that day, and he was cut about the face.

There were two other adults in the Donlon house at the time of the alleged murder. One was a Mr. Thomas McGuire, a laborer. He would testify that he was sitting behind the stove at the time and that he was "pretty drunk" and did not get up from where he was sitting. He said he heard Mrs. Donlon say that Gates did not have any business coming there to abuse her husband. Since he did not leave his seat, he didn't know who else was in the room, and he didn't touch Gates.

The second adult, Mr. Patrick O'Rourke, was boarding with the Donlons and on that evening was upstairs in bed. He said that he heard Mrs. Donlon ask Gates what brought him into the house, saying, "Have you come to murder my lawful husband in his own house?" Gates replied with a derogatory remark, to which Mrs. Donlon replied, "You rascal, leave the house." At that point, O'Rourke said he fell down the stairs, striking his head on the sill. By the time he entered the room, both Gates and Donlon were lying on the floor. Gates had his hand on Donlon's throat and one in his hair. Donlon had one arm across Gates's chest and the other hand in Gates's hair. He claims he did not see any blows and that he parted the men and Mrs. Donlon.

Mr. Sherman happened to be passing by the Barnum-Donlon house on that fateful November evening. He did not live in the Village of Honeoye Falls, but he knew Gates and Donlon by sight. As he passed by, he heard two women come out of that house and say that "they" were killing Bill Gates. "They asked me to go in and stop them," he said, "but I did not go." He said he heard a sound like chopping meat and looked through the lattice. Sherman said he "saw a person, raising an instrument and striking. The weapon looked like a half circle as it came up." He could not tell who was holding it, but he did see three blows struck. He did not hear any words, and he did not know who was being hit. About two minutes later, he saw Barnum pull Gates out onto the steps and sit him up. "I noticed a free flow of blood about the size of my finger. I went up and spoke to Gates three or four times without an answer. I asked if I should go for a doctor, and Barnum said I should." Sherman said that he saw a woman in the door but did not look inside the house, as he was about six feet from the door and "didn't like the business." He also stated that he saw Barnum first come out of the house and pace back and forth in front of the door before going back in and pulling Gates out. "I did see Gates later at the doctor's," said Sherman. "He had five ugly wounds."

There remained four individuals who still had to weigh in on the events of the night of November 8. There is no record that Gates said anything pertaining to the event in the ten days that he lay dying from his wounds. Mrs. Gates was not present at the Donlons when the beating occurred. According to Mrs. Gates, Mrs. Donlon had threatened her husband after Mr. Donlon was discharged from the railroad. Mrs. Gates claimed that Mrs. Donlon said she would have Gates's heart's blood if she had to go up to her knees to get it. She claimed to have heard threats like these up to three days before the assault. She did not see her husband until later that evening at the doctor's office when the doctor was dressing his wounds. "His face was covered with blood, one eye cut to pieces; his nose cut off and his face all cut to pieces," she said. Gates lingered for ten days before finally succumbing to his injuries. During that time, Mrs. Gates said that he was conscious for two days, then semiconscious for the next three and unconscious for the last four days before he died. She claimed that after the first night, the family did not leave his bedside until he died on November 18, 1869.

There was no doubt that William Gates had suffered a beating at the hands of Mr. and Mrs. Donlon and that he eventually died of the injuries received in that beating. The question remains: how did that beating come about? Was Gates an innocent victim of hatred and revenge, or had he, in fact, precipitated the fight and simply got the worst of it? The Gates and Barnum families put the blame squarely on the Donlons. That is not Donlons' version of what happened.

"I was sitting at the stove between 6:00 and 7:00 p.m. on the eighth of November; we were talking about killing a pig. No other word was spoken except about killing the pig," said John Donlon, recounting the events of November 8.

> Gates came to the door, opened it and said, "I heard you called my woman a _____." I said I had not, and he says, "You are a liar." I said it is better for you to go home. "Damn you," says Gates, "You ought to be licked and I'll lick you." Gates seized me by the throat and with the other hand struck me and then grabbed me by the hair. He struck me again in the breast and then called Mrs. Donlon a God damned w----; then Gates struck Mrs. Donlon and knocked her against the stove. We both struck each other, and we fell to the floor, then O'Rourke came out and separated us. When Gates knocked Mrs. Donlon over against the stove, she struck him with the stove iron. Don't know how many times.

According to Donlon, Mrs. Barnum wasn't there until Gates was pulled out of the house. He did not recall Mrs. Barnum crying, "Murder!"

There was no doubt that there was animosity between himself and Gates, but not over being discharged. Donlon claimed that he had not been discharged by Gates and that he had voluntarily left the job. He also claimed that on one occasion he met Gates on the tracks on the Honeoye Falls Railroad Bridge. He did not speak to Gates, but Gates said to him, "I don't want you to walk that track, you damned Irishman." Donlon also said that about fifteen minutes before Gates entered his house, he had had an altercation with Barnum in the barn they shared behind the house. At that time, Donlon admitted that he had kicked Barnum after Barnum hit him with a shovel, leaving him blind in one eye.

Barnum had been home when Gates arrived and left before Gates went next door to the Donlons'. It is easy to surmise that Barnum would have told Gates of the altercation in the barn. So it is possible that between that and Gates's obvious dislike of Donlon, he might have instigated the entire affair.

It was Mrs. Donlon whom everyone in the house, including herself, claimed hit Gates in the face with something iron from the stove. She said she was in the buttery when she heard Gates ask Donlon if he had called his wife names. She heard her husband ask Gates to leave and claimed Gates responded that he would not leave until he licked Donlon. She said she screamed, "Murder! Did you come to murder my lawful husband?" When Gates got ahold of Donlon, she also caught ahold of her husband, and

New York Central Railroad covered bridge over Honeoye Creek, taken 1880. *Author's collection.*

Gates struck her on the temple, leaving a mark that was visible the next day. She recounted that "Gates had Donlon by the throat and hair; I picked up something from the stove and struck Gates three times. I was much excited and thought Gates was going to kill my husband." She claimed that she said nothing about killing; she said she did not strike Gates as Barnum was drawing him out of the house and had no intention of killing him.

There was one more witness to the event on November 8. That person was William "Willie" Donlon, the Donlons' fourteen-year-old son. He was questioned by the coroner and both the counsel for the defense and for the prosecution. He was behind the door when Gates came in. His parents were talking about killing a pig when the door opened and Gates entered, saying, "Donlon, what are you calling my wife names for?" Willie said his father denied it, and Gates called him a "God damn liar." "Donlon told Gates to leave and tried to shut the door," Willie said, "but Gates caught him by the throat and struck him." Donlon then knocked Gates down, and while they were on the floor, his mother came in and, after asking Gates if he had come to kill her husband, struck him with something on the head four or five times before O'Rourke pulled her off.

The Donlons were arrested the day after, on November 9, and charged with murder. They were later released on bail to await trial. A.D.J. MacDonald, a Honeoye Falls lawyer, would represent them. He saw Mr. and Mrs. Donlon the next day. "I noticed a lump on her [Mrs. Donlon's] forehead. It was quite a bruise, the flesh discolored and somewhat inflamed. There were scratches on either side of Donlon's neck and bruises on the side of his head." Living in the village, MacDonald had on more than one occasion heard the threats that Gates made to Donlon and vice versa. He had heard Gates's remark to Donlon on one occasion: "Damn you, if you don't keep out of my way I'll fix you."

At the trial beginning on November 15, 1869, the attorneys for the defense argued that the action of Donlon was justifiable in that he was repelling a violent attack and therefore was not guilty. "Donlon was in his own house," said Judge Chumasero. "The place was sacred; its freedom and sanctity guaranteed to them by every principle of law. It was Gates who opened the door and entered." He also argued that Mrs. Donlon's actions were justifiable, as the law permits a wife to kill an assailant in defense of her husband. In addition, Chumasero argued that Gates was the instigator and that Donlon was defending himself and his wife, and she him. He claimed that "every particle of the evidence of the affair had come from the Barnum family, and they were as incompetent to give evidence as Donlon and his wife." He concluded that the only reasonable verdict would be justifiable homicide.

Mr. Davison, the district attorney, presented the case for the prosecution. Gates and Donlon were well acquainted. Donlon had once worked on the railroad and had been discharged by Gates. There was animosity between the two. On the night in question, Gates heard some expression from Donlon's side of the house, relative to Gates's wife. Gates entered Donlon's apartment asking why Donlon had called his wife names; Donlon denied doing that. Words were exchanged between the two men, and Donlon threw Gates down. While Gates was lying on the floor, Mrs. Gates struck him with a stove griddle and some other weapon, "horribly chopping his face and head, all the while crying, 'Kill him; kill him!'" Gates's death was the result of the beating inflicted by the Donlons. He asked for a verdict of guilty of murder.

Judge Johnson explained the law as it affected the case and said the jury could find a verdict of murder in the first or second degree; justifiable homicide; or manslaughter in one of its degrees. He told the jurors that they must "canvass the whole testimony and render their verdict on the evidence according to their oaths." The jury went out at fifty minutes after four o'clock and returned at six o'clock that evening, rendering an "unqualified verdict of murder in the second degree." Apparently, it took only two votes for the jury to decide the verdict. It was reported in the *Rochester Union and Advertiser*

Above: Sing Sing Prison, Ossining, New York, date unknown. *Courtesy of the Library of Congress, Washington, D.C.*

Left: Sing Sing Prison cell in Ossining, New York, circa 1910. *Courtesy of the Library of Congress, Washington, D.C.*

that on the first ballot, the jury stood eight for second-degree murder, two for manslaughter in the second degree and two for the third degree. After more discussion, the second ballot found the jurors unanimous for a verdict of murder in the second degree.

The Donlons were sentenced on February 21, 1870, the day after the trial ended. John Donlon, who was sixty-one years old, was sentenced to life in the state prison in Auburn, New York. His wife, Catherine, thirty-nine years old, was sentenced to fifteen years in Sing Sing Prison. They were both transported to their respective prisons on February 26, 1870. John Donlon died in Auburn Prison on July 4, 1877, from "abscess of the liver and scirrhus [*sic*]." Catherine served her sentence and was released in 1885. She was returned to the Rochester Almshouse. No record of her after that has been found.

That might have been the end of the story had it not been for the fact that the Donlons had six children: John Edward, William "Willie," Daniel, Frank, Sarah and Peter. The children were originally sent to the Rochester Orphan Asylum. The fate of children in the Orphan Asylum was adoption, indenture, aging out at sixteen or, unfortunately, death. No records could be found at the asylum for William and John, but through genealogical searches, it is believed that they made their way to Colorado, lived and worked with an uncle and eventually died there. Frank was taken in by a local family, as was Peter.

Sarah's fate was the only one found in the Orphan Asylum records. In 1874, at the age of eight, she was indentured to a Mr. Henry Calwell. The indenture would expire when she turned eighteen, in 1883. However, she was taken from Mr. Calwell on account of "ill treatment." She was next taken by Mrs. Haight and returned about a year later as "unmanageable." She was then taken by a Mrs. Bogman for a short time but again returned, and in 1877, she was taken for the last time by Mrs. Hale. She disappeared from Mrs. Hale's and was gone for about six months. She returned, saying that she had been enticed into a convent and kept there in confinement. It wasn't long before she again left Mrs. Hale. The last record in the asylum records states that she was leading a "roving life," and it was not known what became of her. A family letter indicated that she was living in Baltimore, Maryland, in 1880.

The case of Gates and Donlon is a sorry tale. It is difficult to believe that justice was done. There was no doubt that Gates was killed by the Donlons, but was it, indeed, murder or a case of justifiable homicide?

7

Murder at the Junction

Murder of Spencer Howe, August 19, 1894

Rochester Junction, also known as "the Junction," was the place where the Lehigh Valley Railroad and the Rochester–Hemlock branch joined together in the Town of Mendon. It was a bustling place where passengers from Rochester trains had to change for main-line destinations like New York City, Buffalo, Chicago and Detroit. At its peak, seven or eight trains each way, every day, shuttled passengers and carried produce and coal and, in the early 1900s, immigrants seeking jobs out west. To accommodate passengers and workers, a hotel and livery stable were built. There were also shanties built to accommodate the immigrant laborers who, in 1894, were hired to begin work on the Hemlock Lake water conduit.

In 1894, the immigrants who were working on the Hemlock Lake conduit and living in the shanties at the Junction were Italians. These men left their homes and families to earn a living, the fruits of which many of them sent back to Italy. Some of them would stay until they earned sizeable sums, and then they would return to Italy. Others saved their money to bring their families to this country to start new lives. The point is that all of the workers in the camp were men. They worked all week—possibly six out of seven days—and if they were not saving their money, they spent it on drink. In camps like this one, there was always someone to supply the drink. At Rochester Junction, that person was Pete Vandetto. Pete served beer illegally, as he had no license in his shanty. It was not unusual for a disagreement or even a fight to break out among the men drinking in Pete's shanty. On Easter Sunday, March 24, 1894, such a fight occurred, and this time someone was killed.

Rochester Junction railroad yards, Town of Mendon, New York, taken circa 1900. *Author's collection.*

The scene of the murder of Spencer Howe—shanty at Rochester Junction. *From the* Rochester Union and Advertiser, *March 26, 1894. Reprinted courtesy of the Rochester Public Library, Rochester, New York.*

Spencer Howe, the murdered man. *From the* Rochester Union and Advertiser, *March 26, 1894. Reprinted courtesy of the Rochester Public Library, Rochester, New York.*

Spencer Howe was a transfer agent employed by the United States Express Company at the Junction. He had only been on the job about one year. He, his wife and their young child lived in one of the Sheldon houses at the Junction. Howe had been known in the neighborhood as a powerful man who seldom went into a fight without coming out on top. From all accounts, he was well liked by the Italian workers, but on that Easter Sunday afternoon, March 24, 1894, he was killed by a stiletto blade plunged into his upper thigh, severing his femoral artery. There was a murder at the Junction.

So how did the supposedly well-liked young man end up dead? According to the *Rochester Union and Advertiser*, at 3:30 p.m., George Ketchum, brother-in-law of Howe, was in Pete's shanty drinking beer with a group of Italians who by that time were intoxicated. A fight broke out between Ketchum and at least one of the Italians. Howe, hearing that his brother-in-law was in a fight and getting the worst of it, went to the shanty to help him. Howe was able to free his brother-in-law, who ran out of the shanty as a group of Italians swarmed Howe. One of them had a stiletto and stabbed Howe in the leg. Howe staggered out of the shanty and down the hill toward the railroad tracks. He fell facedown in the mud and died. Four hours later, Howe's body was found in a pool of blood near the railroad tracks. An alarm was sounded, and the constable from Honeoye Falls and the sheriff of the county were sent for. Deputy Harnish of Honeoye Falls arrived first and took charge of the case. Sheriff Hannan arrived by train the next day. A witness, Edward Mullen, a worker on the conduit, thought he saw an Italian, Nicolo DeNardo, with a knife. Upon hearing that, Deputy Harnish began a search for DeNardo and his friends.

Above: Freight house at Rochester Junction, Town of Mendon, where Spencer Howe was employed. *Photo by B. Fanghanel, 1999.*

Right: Nicolo DeNardo, accused of murder. *From the* Rochester Union and Advertiser, *March 26, 1894. Reprinted courtesy of the Rochester Public Library, Rochester, New York.*

Nicolo DeNardo was a short, thickset Italian about forty years of age. He had a scar under his right eye, and he was partially bald. He had only been in the United States for about a year and had been working at the Junction for the last three months. There had been three other Italians with him in Pete's Shanty—Antonio DeNiclio, Camillo Geantomaso and Rocco DeFilippo. By the time Howe's body had been discovered and Deputy Harnish went to look for and question them, they were nowhere to be found. Their descriptions were sent to Caledonia, where DeNardo was believed to have a cousin. Descriptions were also sent to Rochester, as it was not uncommon for immigrants suspected of crimes to try to make their way back to New York City to board a ship for Italy and to safety. A reward of $100 was offered for the capture of DeNardo and $25 for his three friends.

The next day, while the search for the four Italians went on, the coroner held an inquest at Dunker's Tavern at the Junction. It was determined that Howe bled to death due to a severed femoral artery made by a blade cutting a one-inch-wide and four-inch-deep wound in his upper left thigh. Testimony from two witnesses, Peter Vandetto, owner of the shanty, and Ed Mullen, a worker on the conduit, claimed that DeNardo had a knife. With that testimony, the coroner's jury ruled that Howe was murdered, and DeNardo and his three friends— DeNiclio, Geantomaso and DeFilippo—were the culprits.

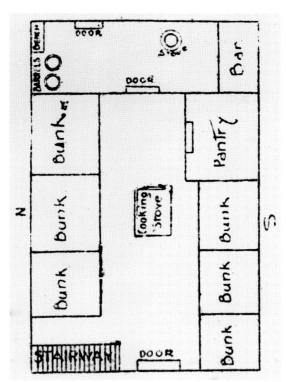

Interior of the shanty at Rochester Junction. *From the* Rochester Union and Advertiser, *March 26, 1894. Reprinted courtesy of the Rochester Public Library, Rochester, New York.*

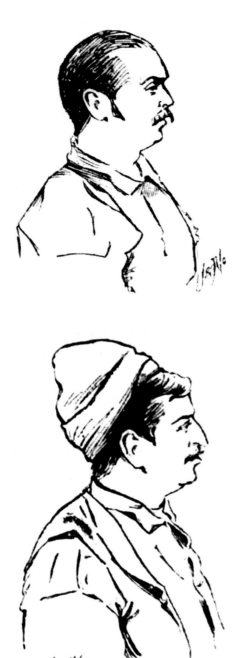

Above, left: Antonio DeNiclio. *From the* Rochester Union and Advertiser, *March 28, 1894. Reprinted courtesy of the Rochester Public Library, Rochester, New York.*

Above, right: Camillo Geantomaso. *From the* Rochester Union and Advertiser, *March 28, 1894. Reprinted courtesy of the Rochester Public Library, Rochester, New York.*

Left: Rocco DeFilippo. *From the* Rochester Union and Advertiser, *March 28, 1894. Reprinted courtesy of the Rochester Public Library, Rochester, New York.*

The following day, March 27, Sheriff Hannan, who was confident that the wanted Italians were being sheltered by their countrymen, received a telegram suggesting that he search the shanties about two and a half miles north of the Junction. Waiting until dark, the sheriff and his men surrounded the shanty. Finding an unlatched window, the sheriff entered the shanty and found about sixty sleeping Italians. The men searched the shanty, carefully going from bunk to bunk, and finally found three of the wanted Italians hiding under bunks. They did not find DeNardo.

The three Italians, DeNiclio, Geantomaso and DeFilippo, were taken to Honeoye Falls, arraigned before Justice Burberry and charged with first-degree murder. "They are not accessories to DeNardo's crime, but by their actions in murderously assaulting Howe, if they did as charged, have rendered themselves liable to pay the penalty with death," stated Assistant District Attorney Hanford. "Charge them with murder in the first degree," ordered Judge Burberry. When Mr. Elliott, interpreter for the Italians, who spoke little or no English, translated the charge for the defendants, they shrugged their shoulders and answered, "Not guilty." Asked if they had a lawyer to represent them, the Italians replied that they were too poor, but maybe their friends would assist them; after all, they had been in the United States only one year. They were then remanded to jail in Rochester to await trial.

Once in Rochester, the three Italians were housed in adjoining cells in the Monroe County Jail. Since they spoke almost no English, an interpreter, John Colucci of Rochester, was brought in to talk to the Italians. They denied all knowledge of the affair. Asked why they had fled if they didn't know anything, they replied that they were told to do so by the other Italians; they were told if they didn't run away, they would be in trouble.

In the week following the Howe stabbing, Sheriff Hannan made repeated efforts to capture DeNardo. He traveled around the surrounding towns and counties, visiting Italian shanties and putting local constables on the lookout for DeNardo. By doing so, he made a circle around DeNardo, making it impossible for him to escape to Canada and the Northwest, which was believed to be DeNardo's plan. Sheriff Hannan also worked closely with Paul Elliott, an Italian interpreter, who was able to convince DeNardo's friends to give him up. DeNardo's friends planned to turn him over to Elliott and the sheriff, but DeNardo was captured before they were able to do so. DeNardo was captured about twelve o'clock on Sunday night, April 1, at a shanty near the Erie Railroad station in Caledonia.

Between the time of the stabbing and his capture, DeNardo had followed the railroad tracks and hid under the bridge over the Genesee River between

Caledonia and Rochester. It was reported by the *Rochester Union and Advertiser* that he was accompanied by his nephew, Francois, and a friend, Dominica Testa, for part of the way. After they parted company, DeNardo made his way to a shanty by the Buffalo, Rochester and Pittsburgh Railway (BR&P) tracks near Mumford, where his brother reportedly lived. He hid there for a day and night. On Tuesday, he hid in a barn belonging to a farmer named Cramer that was near the shanty. A *Rochester Union and Advertiser* reporter who interviewed a friend of Mr. Cramer after DeNardo had been sighted in the area on Wednesday said that he and Cramer were getting out a load of hay for the market and their fork touched a man who lay three feet under the hay. The man jumped up and, without a word, walked out of the barn and toward the swamp. Unfortunately, Mr. Cramer had not seen the picture of DeNardo, nor had he read the accounts of the murder at the Junction in the *Rochester Union and Advertiser*, so he regarded the man in his barn as a tramp. The rest of the week before his capture, DeNardo hid in the swamp by day and in either the barn or shanty by night.

DeNardo refused to make any statement at the time of his capture other than "not guilty." He was arraigned in Honeoye Falls before Judge Burberry and charged with first-degree murder, then remanded to the Monroe County Jail to await trial with the three other Italians.

The grand jury in Rochester was the next stop for the defendants. After hearing the evidence presented by the prosecution, the grand jury found no indictment against the three Italians—Antonio DeNiclio, Camillo Geantomaso or Rocco DeFilippo—and they were released. It did hand down an indictment for first-degree murder against DeNardo.

The trial of Nicolo DeNardo began on Monday, June 11, in the Court of Oyer and Terminer in Rochester. Judge Davy presided. Fred Hanford and David Forsyth represented the prosecution, and Bartholomew Keeler represented DeNardo. According to the *Rochester Union and Advertiser*, it would be "one of the shortest murder trials on record."

District Attorney Hanford's main job was to establish that it was actually DeNardo who stabbed Howe. The first witness for the prosecution was Pete Vandetto. He was the proprietor of the shanty where the stabbing was alleged to have taken place. He testified that Howe and Ketchum were in the shanty before the Italians arrived. "Ketchum and the Italians were wrestling," he said. "Howe wanted to show them how to wrestle in this country, but I told them, 'Boys, stop fooling around.'" He went on to testify that when Ketchum knocked one of the Italians down, he got angry. "I saw DeNardo take what I thought was a knife out of his pocket, and I threw him out of the door and told them all to get out. I got them out and shut the door," he said. He was unable to state for sure whether DeNardo actually had a knife, and he did not see DeNardo stab Howe.

The next witness for the prosecution was William Griffin, another worker on the water conduit. He, too, was in the shanty along with Ketchum and Howe and, in his words, "nearly twenty Italians." He concurred with Vandetto that the Italians and Ketchum were wrestling and that Ketchum knocked down an Italian. "I saw blood on the Italian's face," he said. He went on to testify that he saw a knife and a razor in the hands of two of the Italians, but when asked if he could identify any of them, he replied he could not because "they all look so near alike." He did remember seeing a small pool of blood on the floor, and he was able to identify DeNardo as the one who shut the shanty door after Pete told them to get out.

George Ketchum, Howe's brother-in-law, was the next to testify. He, too, was unable to identify DeNardo as one of the men in the scuffle in the shanty. In fact, he was unable to swear that he had ever seen DeNardo prior to his capture. He did admit that he and Howe had been drinking and that Howe was showing the Italians some wrestling moves. "Howe started to show one of them [the Italians] some grips in wrestling. The Italian was thrown down, and he got up mad. There was a scuffle, and some of the Italians began to draw their knives," he testified. He went on to say that he knocked down one of the Italians, who had either pulled out a knife or razor on his way out of the shanty. He claimed that Howe had left before him and had gone down the tracks. He did not follow him but instead went to Howe's house and told Howe's wife and his mother about the scuffle. He said he was going to go back to the shanty, but the women urged him not to go, so he went home. "I did not know of Howe's death until the next day," he said.

The testimonies of only two prosecution witnesses implicated DeNardo in the killing. The first was Pietro Sarafino, who swore that DeNardo was the only one in the crowd around Howe with a knife. He said, "DeNardo was pushing and shoving Howe at the door," but Sarafino did not see DeNardo actually stab Howe. Angelo Fenditto was the only one to testify that he saw DeNardo actually strike at Howe's legs with a knife. Following their testimony, the prosecution rested its case.

Mr. Keeler, attorney for DeNardo, moved to have the charges against DeNardo dismissed on the grounds that no evidence had been produced to show that DeNardo was, in fact, guilty of the crime. Keeler told the court, "There is nothing to fasten the crime on him any more than there is to convict any of the others who were engaged in the row." Unfortunately,

Judge Davy did not agree. He replied to Keeler, "I think I will let the jury dispose of the case."

On the second day of the trial, Mr. Keeler, attorney for DeNardo, presented his defense by putting his only witness, Nicolo DeNardo, on the stand. Since he spoke very little English, DeNardo testified with the aid of an interpreter. He began by admitting that he was in the shanty that Sunday afternoon. Asked if he had been drinking, he replied, "I had drunk only two glasses of beer. I can't drink much beer." When asked if he knew Ketchum and Howe, he replied that he did not know Ketchum but that he had seen Howe around the Lehigh Valley Depot but had never spoken to him. He admitted that he had been scuffling with the rest of the Italians but that he had not struck anyone:

> I did not have a knife with me that day. It was old, and I didn't often carry it. I did not strike Howe. Someone shoved me out of the door in the rush, but I don't know who it was. After I was put out, I did not see Howe or Ketchum; neither did I see them run down the railroad tracks. I did not know Howe was dead until Pete Vandetto told me and said, "My son we'll all go to prison for this." Pete didn't say anything about my being arrested for the killing, and no one came after me that day.

Bartholomew Keeler summed up the case for the defense first by discussing the testimony of the physicians who had examined Howe's wounds. He argued that the wounds could not have been inflicted by the small, short-bladed knife that belonged to DeNardo and had been offered into evidence as the murder weapon. "Does it look reasonable that this little knife could penetrate the trousers and underclothes of the victim and inflict a wound nearly six inches in length?" he asked. He then went on to claim that Ketchum and Howe had no business being in the shanty and that it was Ketchum who had induced Howe into making the fatal visit. "There would have been no row in the shanty had these two men not been there," stated Keeler. He also pointed out that no one had actually seen DeNardo stab Howe. David Forsyth summed up the case for the prosecution.

Before dismissing the jury to deliberate, Judge Davy charged the jury, saying:

> You should not convict the defendant upon mere suspicion, however strong it may be, or simply because there is a strong belief that he is guilty. No person saw the defendant strike a blow. One of the Italians claims he saw a knife but did not see the defendant strike. All of the other witnesses failed to see

this. All the testimony rests on one individual who saw him make a motion to strike a blow but saw no knife. If it had not been for this, I would not have hesitated in discharging the prisoner and would not have submitted the case to your consideration. Should you come to the conclusion, from all the evidence, facts and circumstances in the case, that some other person had the same opportunity to stab the deceased as the defendant had and that all the circumstances point as clearly to some other person having stabbed the deceased as the defendant, then these facts are sufficient to raise a reasonable doubt as to the guilt of the defendant.

The jury was then dismissed to deliberate. It was late in the afternoon on June 13. The trial had lasted two days.

The jury was out all night. The *Rochester Union and Advertiser* reported that on the first ballot, the jurors voted nine to three for acquittal. The three who voted against thought that DeNardo was sufficiently implicated and that he should be convicted of manslaughter. The second ballot, at about midnight, produced a similar result, but this time only two held out for manslaughter. An agreement was reached shortly before the court convened in the morning of June 14. As the jury entered the courtroom, DeNardo, who was seated next to his counsel, nervously scanned the jurors' faces as they took their seats. Although he understood little English, DeNardo caught the meaning of the words "not guilty," and his face immediately brightened with smiles and tears. Judge Davy discharged DeNardo, who was then surrounded by his numerous countrymen who were in the court awaiting the verdict.

Following his acquittal, Nicolo DeNardo returned to his former place on the conduit. A short time later, the contractor in charge of that section was confronted by a delegation of Italians. The leader of the Italians protested in the name of his fellow countrymen against allowing DeNardo to work with them. There is no information about whether DeNardo was let go, if he found other work or if, in fact, he returned to Italy.

Bartholomew Keeler, DeNardo's defense attorney, asked Judge Davy to award him $1,200 for his services in defending DeNardo. Keeler made his application under a new law that counsel employed by order of the court to defend a prisoner who is unable to hire an attorney might apply to the court for such compensation to which, as in the discretion of the court, he is entitled. In his application, Keeler enumerated the amount of time and labor that he expended in preparing DeNardo's defense. He called the court's attention to the fact that the defendant and almost all of the witnesses in the case were unacquainted with the English language, requiring him to hire an interpreter to make their testimony intelligible to the jury. This marks the beginning, at least in this small part of the country, of our current law that states that if a person accused of a crime cannot afford a lawyer, one will be appointed for him by the court and paid by such.

Judge Davy reserved his decision on Keeler's application since this was the first of its kind to be presented under the new law and he wished to examine it more closely and consult with his associates before making a decision.

8

Money Mayhem

Counterfeiting in the Village, September 2, 1903

At the turn of the century, paper money, as we know it, was not as common as it is now. Most people didn't have much money at all, and what they did have was mostly coins, not only quarters, dimes and nickels, but also silver dollars, five-dollar gold pieces and ten-dollar gold pieces. When we commonly think of counterfeiting money, we think of paper money and printing (even Xerox copying), but in 1903, in a rambling old house on isolated Hyde Street in Honeoye Falls (now Hyde Park), counterfeiting of coins was being done.

William Atkinson came to Honeoye Falls from Oswego, New York. He married Susan, a resident of the village, and they moved to a two-story house on Hyde Street. It was a picturesque spot across the street from Honeoye Creek. The rambling old house was built for two families, one on each side. Years before, it could have been a tavern, since the rooms on the ground floor were large, and a central staircase gave access to rooms on the upper floor. Unfortunately, it was a neglected house. Many of the rooms were unused. What furniture there was was old and plain, and the house had a musty smell like one that had been closed up for some time. Some of the windows had no curtains.

Atkinson was fifty years old. At the time of his arrest for counterfeiting, he was employed at the paper mill in the village, but he actually was not much of a workingman. He preferred the easy life of hunting and fishing. His wife, Susan, was the breadwinner of the family. She worked at a hotel in the village. Additional income came from having a boarder in the house, Millard Whitbeck, a man approximately thirty-five years old.

Atkinson House on Hyde Street (now Hyde Park), Honeoye Falls, New York. *Author's collection.*

On September 1, 1903, United States deputy marshal Robert Burns of Rochester received a telephone tip from an unknown informant that "underhanded work" was going on in the Village of Honeoye Falls. The informant did not give specifics about exactly what the "underhanded work" was. At the same time, counterfeit coins were showing up in the city of Rochester, and there was a report of someone displaying large quantities of silver coins in Honeoye Falls. When all of this information reached United States commissioners Edwin C. Smith and Delbert C. Hebbard, they sent Detective Daniel Scholl to Honeoye Falls with orders to investigate—in particular, to check out a suspicious house on Hyde Street.

Detective Scholl arrived in Honeoye Falls, proceeding immediately to the house under suspicion on Hyde Street. He found five dogs running loose about the place, but there was no one at home, and there were no signs that that house was even occupied. His initial search of the property apparently gave him sufficient evidence to obtain an official search warrant for the property and an arrest warrant for the residents. With this evidence, Scholl telephoned Commissioners Smith and Hebbard requesting that they have Deputy Burns meet him at their office when he arrived on the late train to Rochester.

At the meeting with Smith, Hebbard and Burns, Scholl reported on what he had found, and a search warrant was issued for the Hyde Street house, as well as arrest warrants for the three residents of the house, William Atkinson; Sarah, his wife; and Millard Whitbeck, their boarder. With these documents in hand, Scholl, Deputy Burns and Secret Service Agent Sheehan went to Honeoye Falls the next day to make the arrests and carry out the search warrant.

Upon arriving at the house on Hyde Street, they again found no one at home. They immediately gained entrance to the house and commenced their search for molds, dies and other tools used to counterfeit coins. In a woodshed at the back of the house they found money in an old cupboard—about fifteen dollars' worth of dimes, quarters, halves and dollars. With this, the officers decided that it would be best to arrest the counterfeiters as soon as possible, so they left the house to inquire about where they might be found. Leaving a deputy to watch the place, they went to the paper mill, where they were told Atkinson was employed. They arrested him and took him to the village lock-up. They learned that Whitbeck was supposedly fishing at Mendon Ponds. Deputy Burns, along with a man who could identify Whitbeck, was sent to arrest him, but before they left, they learned that, in fact, Whitbeck was in the village.

Constable Druschel was directed to find and arrest him. Sheehan and Scholl remained at the house in case Whitbeck returned. As luck would have it, Constable Druschel had gone about "forty rods" up the road when he met Whitbeck returning home. "Hello," Druschel said. "There are a couple of men down at the house who want to see you, Whitbeck." When Whitbeck reached the house, he was immediately placed under arrest and searched. Counterfeit coins were found in his possession. He, too, was confined in the village lock-up. Meanwhile, the officers went to the hotel where Sarah Atkinson worked. She was arrested and taken to the village lock-up as well.

After arresting the alleged counterfeiters, the officers returned to the house to resume their search. Drawers were ransacked, mattresses were pulled off beds and ripped open and pictures were taken down in search of hiding places in the walls. They found tools, metal and molds for making the bogus coins. The molds were made by pressing a genuine coin into wet plaster of Paris. The coin left a nice impression in the plaster as it hardened. An impression of the other side of the coin was also made, and the two were put together and fastened with a vice to complete the mold. A small hole bored into the edge of the two half-molds permitted hot lead to be poured in, filling the mold. Once hardened and cooled, the coin was removed from the mold and smoothed, polished and milled. A machine for polishing the coins consisting of a lathe made from an old sewing machine frame with felt rolls on a revolving

Honeoye Falls Village Hall and Lockup. *Courtesy of Honeoye Falls/Mendon Historical Society.*

shaft made from bicycle gears and run by foot power was also found. In a writing desk in what would be considered the living room, the officers found several unfinished counterfeit coins of different denominations. All of this was confiscated and taken back to Rochester as evidence.

The suspected counterfeiters, Sarah and William Atkinson and Millard Whitbeck, were also taken to Rochester and arraigned before Marshal Hebbard. They were held on $5,000 bail and placed in the Monroe County Jail. A hearing date was set for September 5.

Marshal Hebbard was greatly elated over the capture. "There has been altogether too much counterfeit money floating around this part of the state of late, and I have strong hopes that this round-up will be of great benefit in relieving this evil," he said. This was the first time capture of counterfeiters had taken place in the Rochester area for several years.

The September 5 hearing was held in the Federal Building in Rochester in the office of Deputy Marshal Burns. William Atkinson was represented by Philetus Chamberlain, and John D. Lynn represented Millard Whitbeck. There were only four witnesses from Honeoye Falls present: Florence Lathrop, Raleigh Holden, James Brown and James Donnelly. Following the hearing, Atkinson and Whitbeck were held for the grand jury. Susan Atkinson, who was first thought to be an accomplice, was not held but discharged soon after her arrest. She was illiterate and did not know the denominations of the money, so Commissioner Smith was satisfied that the woman was innocent of any wrongdoing.

On November 11, 1903, Atkinson and Whitbeck were tried before Judge Hazel in a federal court in Buffalo. They were found guilty of counterfeiting. Atkinson was sentenced to two years and three months in Auburn Prison and a fine of $250. Whitbeck was sentenced to two years in Auburn Prison and a fine of $150. Atkinson could be eligible for parole in 1906 and Whitbeck in late 1905.

After serving his sentence, Atkinson was released, but there is no information about what became of him. Whitbeck, on the other hand, apparently returned to the area. He married Rose Quandt and fathered three children. The 1920 state census has him listed as the head of a household in the neighboring Town of Victor, and in 1930, he was living in Farmington. According to family records, he died on July 9, 1937, in Canandaigua but is buried in an unmarked grave in Mendon Cemetery.

Whitbeck did not live what would be described as "an uneventful life" after his arrest and incarceration for counterfeiting. In 1914, while living in Lima, a town only three-quarters of mile south of the Village of Honeoye Falls, Whitbeck shot and seriously injured his brother-in-law, Walter Quandt. At the time, Quandt, the brother of Whitbeck's wife, Rose, was living with the Whitbecks. A quarrel between Quandt and Whitbeck erupted over furniture that Quandt, who was moving out, wanted to take with him. Whitbeck refused to let the furniture go, claiming a lien on the property. The quarrel grew heated, and finally Whitbeck pulled out a revolver and shot Quandt in the head near the temple.

Neighbors hearing the shot rushed to the scene and discovered Quandt bleeding from what was thought to be a fatal wound. The coroner of Lima, Haggerty, was called, and Whitbeck was once more placed under arrest, this time charged with assault and possibly manslaughter. Quandt's injury was considered inoperable by the doctors attending him. Unfortunately, the resolution of this case is unknown. What is known is that in 1920, Whitbeck is listed as head of a household in Victor, so if he was found guilty of assault or even manslaughter, he did not spend more than five years—and probably less—in jail.

9

Misses Dog—Kills Wife

The Shooting of Mrs. Johanna Kirschner, August 28, 1909

There are many reasons a person might shoot another: rage, jealously, hatred and money. The killing can be premeditated, spur-of-the-moment or accidental. Some cases are solved quickly; others are solved after months or even years of hard work, and some are never solved at all. The shooting and death of Johanna Kirschner should have been a relatively simple case to solve. Her husband admitted to it. "It was an accident," he said. "I was aiming at the dog." The problem lies in the conflicting evidence and in the testimony at the inquest. Was this really an accident or a case of murder?

Charles Kirschner and his wife, Johanna, had immigrated to this country from Germany. Six months prior to the shooting, they had lived on the farm belonging to Mr. and Mrs. Roumalde Reitze, for whom Kirschner worked. The Reitzes were related to the Kirschners by blood and/or marriage, which probably accounts for the matter-of-fact manner in which they testified about the events of that fateful day. They did not want to say anything that could be used against Mr. Kirschner.

It was a Saturday. According to Fred Bauer, who claimed he was Mrs. Kirschner's uncle and lived on a farm near the Kirschner's home, "Mrs. Kirschner came about eleven o'clock and stayed to dinner. Kirschner, himself, came in while we were at the table. He had one glass of ale and then sat down to dinner with us. After dinner, we all went out on the porch, and in a few minutes Kirschner went away." This was verified by Mr. Roumalde Reitze, Mrs. Kirschner's uncle, but he added that Kirschner left about two o'clock that afternoon, saying he was going to look after the cows in the pasture. Later, at the inquest, when asked by the Assistant Attorney Zimmerman, "When Kirschner left the house after dinner, where did he go?" Mr. Reitze replied, "He went to the barn." So Charles Kirschner had dinner with his relatives and his wife, who got there before him, and after dinner he left to go to either the barn or the pasture. Mrs. Kirschner left about fifteen minutes after her husband, according to the relatives.

Shortly after she left, there was a shot. The shot was heard at the Reitze house by both Fred Bauer and Mr. and Mrs. Reitze. According to Fred Bauer, "It was about two o'clock or perhaps a little after. I heard a shot. Then, in a moment or two, Kirschner came running up to my house crying out that he had shot his wife. He wanted me to get a doctor. I told him I could not run fast enough and that he had better go himself. He then started down the road on a run."

Both Fred Bauer and Mrs. Reitze went to the Kirschner home after hearing the shot. Fred Bauer reported, "We found Mrs. Kirschner lying on the couch. We looked for the injury and, after taking off part of her clothing, put cold water and antiseptics on the wound. Mrs. Kirschner had lost a great deal of blood." Mrs. Reitze said, "I only stayed at his house two or three minutes after the shooting. I told Kirschner it was a careless piece of business." When asked why she said that, she replied, "Well, I didn't know whether it was an accident or not. I thought it was carelessness."

The question now was how did Mr. Kirschner come to shoot his wife? Kirschner said nothing about having dinner at the Reitze farm before the shooting. He said he had been hunting woodchucks, and when he returned, he decided to shoot a little dog that belonged to him and his wife. The dog was in the habit of running away. The dog was tied to a tree in the front yard. Kirschner had a Winchester rifle, and he was aiming at the dog when his wife came out of the front door in range of the gun just as he fired. He carried her into the house and placed her on the couch. He then ran to the Reitze house to report the accident and get help, and from there he ran to A.A. Lord's store in Mendon Center, where he telephoned Dr. White. The call was made about five minutes before three o'clock that afternoon. At the store, Kirschner pressed Fred Wolfberger's automobile into service, and he and Wolfsberger returned to the Kirschner home.

Dr. White arrived at the Kirschner home and pronounced Mrs. Kirschner dead. A call was made to the coroner's office and the sheriff. By that afternoon, representatives of the district attorney and the sheriff arrived to begin an investigation. Photos were taken of the house, and measurements were made of the premises.

Later on that same Saturday afternoon, Kirschner was taken before Justice George A. Stayman in Mendon and questioned by Coroner Killip. It had been reported that Kirschner had been drinking quite a bit of hard cider that day. Coroner Killip began questioning Kirschner, but on the advice of J.P. O'Connor, a Rochester lawyer who lived in Mendon, Kirschner refused to answer any questions. The coroner told Kirschner to appear at the inquest. Kirschner was taken into custody, charged with manslaughter and taken to jail. It was reported in the *Honeoye Falls Times*, a local paper, that while in jail Kirschner was questioned by representatives of the district attorney's office and made statements that did not coincide with those he had made previously.

On Sunday, the day after the "accident," Coroner Killip, along with Drs. B.D. White and Kirk Otis, held an autopsy at the Kirschner home. The wound was made by an .88-caliber ball. It had entered the body at the right hip and passed downward and through the fleshy part of the left thigh, lodging beneath the skin. The bullet was soft-nosed and had flattened out, leaving an ugly wound as it ploughed through and severed the femoral artery. Mrs. Kirschner had bled to death within minutes of having been shot.

The inquest into Mrs. Kirschner's death was begun in the Mendon Town Hall on Thursday morning, September 8, with Coroner Killip presiding and the district attorney's office represented by F.F. Zimmerman. Fred Bauer testified again that the Kirschners had been with him and the Reitzes for dinner, that they had both left afterward and that he had heard a shot followed by Mr. Kirschner asking for help because he had shot his wife. He continued, saying that he had gone to Kirschner's house, where he found Mrs. Kirschner on the couch, and had tried to doctor the wound, but she had lost a lot of blood. Bauer again reiterated that Kirschner had only one glass of ale at the dinner. He stated that at the time of the incident, he did not ask Kirschner how the shooting occurred but that he had heard Kirschner say he had shot his wife: "I never saw anything out of the way with Kirschner and never heard him make any threats against his wife." He knew that Kirschner had a gun and had owned one for twenty years. He also testified that he did not see the gun the day of the shooting, and he did not know if Mrs. Kirschner had any insurance on her life.

The next witness to testify was Mrs. Reitze. She, too, testified that he had only one glass of ale before they sat down to dinner. Asked if Kirschner and his wife had any trouble with regard to his drinking, she replied, "No. He was quick-tempered, and she did not scold him." When asked if she ever saw Kirschner drunk that summer, she replied, "Not very much so. He did pretty well. His wife did not speak about it." She also stated that she had not heard him make any threats against his wife. When asked about the shooting, she replied, "I heard at the time that Kirschner tried to shoot a dog and shot his wife instead. He did not tell me how it happened. He said he did not want to do it and declared that he would have no more comfort in the world." Like Fred Bauer, she claimed she did not see any gun when Kirschner left her house, and she also did not know anything about life insurance.

Mr. Hanford Bushman, of Mendon Center, was the next witness at the inquest. He said he had heard about the accident from his son, who told him that Kirschner had shot his wife. He had gone to the Kirschner house. "Mrs. Reitze told me I should see the wound. I looked at it, and then I looked at the woman's face. I saw at once that the woman was dead, and I told Mrs. Reitze so. I saw the dog tied to a tree with a rope six or seven feet long. It was a small dog, perhaps twelve inches high." He went on to say, "Kirschner was a very good shot. He had killed many woodchucks on my farm." Mr. Bushman testified that he heard Mr. Kirschner say twice, "I shot her, but it was an accident." But he did not hear Kirschner say anything about how the shooting occurred. The district attorney also asked Bushman about Kirschner's drinking. "I would say that he had been drinking that day. As a laboring man, he had a fair reputation."

The last person to testify was Charles Fisher of Mendon, in whose care Kirschner was placed after his arrest. He reported what Kirschner said—that his wife had come out of the front door toward him. "He told her he was going to shoot the dog because he ran away the day before. He said his wife got between him and the dog," said Fisher. "I did tell Kirschner not to drink any more, as I heard that he had been drinking, but after that he did take a drink when I was not looking. He was very nervous and excited. He told me several times that the shooting was an accident. He said he intended to kill the dog, not his wife."

The sheriff and representatives of the district attorney had investigated the scene of the "accident" that Saturday afternoon. They inspected the place where the dog was tied and the place near the pump where Kirschner said he stood when he fired the gun. Kirschner was known to be a good shot. The dog was small, about twelve inches high. Mrs. Kirschner was shot in the right hip. If the shooting had occurred in the manner and at the place Kirschner said, she would have been shot on the left side. Taking all this into consideration, they doubted Kirschner's story that the shooting was an accident. From where he said he stood and based on his shooting ability, they thought it would have been impossible for him to make this kind of mistake.

After hearing all of the witnesses' testimonies, Coroner Killip announced that the inquest would be adjourned to a later date and that the next hearing

Gravestone of Johanna Kirschner, Pittsford Cemetery. *Photo by Vicki Profitt.*

would be held in Rochester. In the meantime, Kirschner was released on bail, pending a decision by the grand jury. The grand jury met on October 16, but the Kirschner case was not brought up. It is assumed that the district attorney did not feel there was enough concrete evidence to charge Kirschner with manslaughter, so the shooting of Mrs. Kirschner remained an "accident."

The funeral of Mrs. Kirschner was held on the Monday following her death. She had no children and was survived by her husband, Charles, and two sisters, Mrs. Keiffer and Mrs. Kramer, both of Rochester. She was buried in the Pittsford Cemetery.

Kirschner was committed to Craig Colony at Groveland, Livingston County, an institution for epileptics at that time. He was listed there until the 1915 census. After that time, and until the 1940 census, he was listed as working on the Albert Farm on Cheese Factory Road in Mendon. Charles Kirschner died on January 26, 1950, of arteriosclerosis. He was buried in the Pittsford Cemetery next to his wife without a gravestone.

10

Love-Lost Murder

The Stefano Affair, September 8, 1910

One of the most commonly used words in any language is the word "love." "Love makes the world go round—it's a many splendored thing." The words "I love you" can make a heart beat faster. It's wonderful, marvelous and sometimes deadly.

Amelia "Melly" Stefano was the sixteen-year-old daughter of John Stefano of Papermill Street in the Village of Honeoye Falls. She was a lovely, dark-haired girl and undoubtedly had many suitors. One such suitor was Luigi Altobelli, a farmhand employed by William Palmer. Luigi had numerous times expressed his love and adoration of the lovely Melly. He had repeatedly asked her to marry him, but each time she responded with a firm no. What was the poor man supposed to do?

Melly spent the summer of 1910 at the home of her uncle Anthony Stefano in Hunts, New York. She returned home in time to start school in September. On the morning of September 8, her father left for work on the railroad in West Bloomfield—the next town south of Honeoye Falls—and her mother decided to take the train into the city of Rochester on some business. Melly was left at home to care for her eighteen-month-old baby sister.

At the train station in Honeoye Falls, Mrs. Stefano happened to run into Luigi. They spoke and rode together until the train reached Rochester Junction, where it made a stop. Luigi excused himself, saying he was going to the smoker, but in fact he left the train. When the train reached Rochester, Mrs. Stefano looked for Luigi, and when she was unable to find him, she had

Stefano House on Paper Mill Street, Honeoye Falls, New York. *Author's collection.*

that mother's intuition that something was not right. She immediately hired an automobile to return to Honeoye Falls.

Meanwhile, Luigi left the train at Rochester Junction and made his way back to Honeoye Falls to the Stefano home. Finding Melly alone, he once again told her of his love for her and asked her to marry him. Again, Melly refused. This time, Luigi did not walk away heart broken. He pulled out a gun. If he could not have her, then no one else would either. He fired four shots at Melly at close range. One of the bullets entered her head near her right eye. A second bullet also entered her head. The third one lodged in her left breast and the last in her left arm. Luigi then left the house and ran into the cornfield, on Papermill Street and disappeared.

Melly was badly injured, having been shot four times, but she was still able to scoop up her eighteen-month-old baby sister. Leaving a bloodied trail, she ran to the house of her neighbor, Mrs. Marasco. There she told her story. Mrs. Marasco immediately notified the sheriff's office and called for a doctor. Drs. Boult and White of the village responded and, after examining Melly, made provisions for her to be removed to the Rochester City Hospital on the 1:25 p.m. train. At that time, Melly was in serious condition, and there was little hope of her recovery.

Officer Courtney of Honeoye Falls, who had been notified along with the sheriff's office, visited the Marasco and Stefano homes shortly after the shooting. He learned that Altobelli, after shooting Melly, had left the house and ran in an easterly direction. He found footprints in the soft earth that led through the cornfield beyond Honeoye Creek toward North Bloomfield. Returning to the village, Officer Courtney enlisted the help of a number of men—among them some prominent men of the village, including Charles Lillibridge, George Maltby, Harry and James O'Brien, F.C. Kent and others—to track down the suspect, Altobelli. Some of the men were armed with rifles. They set out to patrol East Street and North Bloomfield Road, which were adjacent to where the shooting took place. A manhunt was begun.

A mile or so east of the village is a wild spot of wooded country with deep gullies running down to Honeoye Creek. It was here that Altobelli hid himself and was able to evade his pursuers. At about four o'clock in the afternoon, two men of the search party came upon Altobelli hiding beneath some brush with a revolver, taking aim at them. The men decided to back off and get help in order to surround Altobelli. Unfortunately, by the time they returned, Altobelli had slipped away and made his way across a cornfield on the Alex Warren farm.

Meanwhile, Assistant District Attorney Bechtold and Deputy Sheriff Pollock were returning to the Village of Honeoye Falls after having scoured the country roads when they spied a man moving through a cornfield. They immediately started in pursuit. Two or three shots were fired in the air to frighten the fleeing man. The man kept on running into another wooded lot near the Gates farm. Suddenly, a single shot rang out, and the man fell to the ground. When the officers reached the man, they found him with a self-inflicted bullet wound near his temple. He was conscious, with his revolver still in his hand. They had captured Luigi Altobelli.

On their way back into the village, Altobelli, who was conscious, talked with the officers. Reaching the village, he was immediately put aboard a train and taken to Rochester, to the same Rochester City Hospital where Melly was being treated. His injury, like her injuries, was serious. The self-inflicted bullet had imbedded itself in his brain, causing paralysis. A few days later, he died of his wounds, but not before he was visited by Mrs. Stefano, Melly's mother, who reportedly forgave him for shooting her daughter. He was buried in Holy Sepulchre Cemetery in Rochester.

Melly Stefano, though her injuries were considered life threatening and she lost her right eye, did recover. She eventually married Ralph Roberts and had three sons: Eddie, Albert and Charles. Pictures of her always show her

in profile so as to hide the scars of that tragic day. She lived to be seventy-one years of age, and when she died, she was buried in the family plot in St. Paul of the Cross Cemetery in Honeoye Falls along with her husband and sons.

To this day, many of the Stefano family still reside in the Village of Honeoye Falls and the Town of Mendon. Melly's grandson Mike is now a town board member.

Top: Melly Stefano on her wedding day to Ralph Roberts a few years after she was shot. *Courtesy of Michael Roberts.*

Bottom: Gravestone of Melly Stefano Roberts, St. Paul of the Cross Cemetery, Honeoye Falls, New York. *Author's collection.*

11

Ontario Street Murder

Murder of James Duffy, February 18, 1911

Honeoye Falls is one of those friendly, "everyone knows everyone" kind of villages where a knock on a door almost always is answered by a "come on in." In the 1900s, people of the Village of Honeoye Falls might have locked their doors at night, but even that is doubtful. In light of today's high security, with our locked doors with peepholes and sophisticated security systems, not to lock one's doors seems foolish. Maybe if James Duffy had locked his door and looked out before opening it, there would not have been a murder on Ontario Street.

Saturday, February 18, 1911, was a cold winter day. It had snowed the night before, and there were several inches of snow on the ground. By nightfall, most people were holed up in their homes around a warm fire. James Duffy; his granddaughter, seventeen-year-old Verna; and his aged aunt, Elizabeth Webb, were sitting in their parlor. Duffy and his granddaughter were playing cards while the aunt sat by the stove keeping warm. There was a knock on the door. Thinking it was the paperboy, Duffy called out, "Come in."

The door opened and closed, but instead of the local paperboy, a burly black man carrying what would later be described as a "murderous-looking club" entered. The black man asked, "Have you got any money?" Standing up, Duffy replied jokingly, "Lots of it." As Duffy turned, the intruder, without warning, viciously struck him with the club. The blow caught Duffy in the head just over the right eye. As he fell to the floor, his head struck the baseboard a few feet from where his granddaughter Verna had been seated.

Meanwhile, Miss Webb got to her feet and tried to make an escape through the dining room. She was overtaken by the intruder. He struck her with his club. It was a glancing blow to the head that made a wound six inches long and three inches wide. She fell to the floor, dazed.

Verna tried to make her escape the same way as her aunt, but she was also cut off by the intruder. She ran back to the front door and, once out the door, started for the home of a neighbor across the street. The recent snow made her footing unsteady, and she fell. By the time she regained her footing and reached the street, the black man had overtaken her. She struggled with him, but she did not cry out (evidently she was too frightened), so her struggle did not attract the attention of any passersby.

Earl Rittenhouse happened to be passing by a short distance from the struggling girl on his way to his brother's house. It was dark, and he assumed that the struggling girl and the black man were scuffling neighborhood children. He did, however, notice that the two were moving toward the Duffy house and onto the driveway. Dr. Otis was also passing by at that time and saw no reason to be alarmed.

The intruder was pulling Verna toward the wooded lot behind the house. Verna continued to struggle, and four times she managed to break his hold on her. Finally, she succeeded in freeing herself and ran to the home of Jerome Young, where she gave the alarm. Mr. Young called for the village officers and, rounding up other neighbors, returned with Verna to the Duffy house.

Upon arriving at the Duffy house, the neighbors and Verna found Mr. Duffy on the front porch. Evidently, he had at least partially recovered from the blow on the head and had staggered onto the porch. He was covered in blood and unable to talk intelligently about what had happened. He soon lost consciousness and remained unconscious until his death three days later, on February 21.

In the struggle with the intruder, Verna had sustained bite marks to her face, and her right arm had been broken in two places—near the wrist and at the elbow. When she returned home with her neighbors, she immediately began to aid her injured grandfather. By the time Drs. B.R. White and H.S. Benham arrived to tend to the wounded, they found Verna washing blood from her grandfather's face and oblivious to her own injuries, as one arm was hanging helplessly at her side.

When news of what happened at the Duffy home reached the village, Officers Courtney and Druschell were already on the case. They had sent out several groups of people to hunt for the perpetrator and continued to do so through the next morning. Verna had told them that the intruder was a young black man. Johnny Brooks, a young black man from West Bloomfield, immediately fell under suspicion. There were at this time very few black individuals living in Honeoye Falls and the surrounding area. When questioned closely by her uncle Charles, who had rushed to the home when notified of the assault, Verna insisted that the fellow gave his name as Johnny Brooks, but her description of the man did not match the Brooks boy.

Brooks's parents swore that he was home that evening, but to be absolutely certain, Johnny Brooks was brought to the Duffy home on Sunday evening. Verna stated upon seeing him that he was not the man, and he was released at once.

There were two other black men who had been stopping in the village. One of them was boarding with Jesse Hall on North Main Street. Jesse Hall often took in fellow blacks who were in need of a place to stay and helped them find jobs in the area. About eleven o'clock that Saturday night, officers went to Jesse Hall's and asked about the man who was staying there. Hall told the officers that the black man, whose name was James Williams, had been home for supper and had gone to bed early. The officers asked Williams to step outside under the nearest lamppost and carefully examined him for any indication that he had been in a struggle with Verna Duffy. They found none. They then took him to the Duffy home, but Verna was unable to identify him as her attacker. He was released.

On Sunday morning after the crime, Deputy Sheriff Root of Avon, Livingston County, arrived in the village with four other men. The assault and murder, even though it took place within walking distance of the Village of Honeoye Falls, was actually in the next county. Because it was so close to the village and because Mr. Duffy owned a blacksmith business in the village, the neighbors, who thought of themselves as residing in the village, had notified the village officers, who then, in turn, notified the Livingston County Sheriff's Department.

Deputy Sheriff Root first visited the Brooks residence and questioned Johnny Brooks. Once he was satisfied that Brooks was not the right man, his suspicion fell on the stranger staying with Jesse Hall. The deputy sheriff learned that the suspect was in the village on Saturday and was intoxicated. The deputy sheriff asked Williams to accompany him to the Duffy house once more. Williams agreed to go only after he was assured that he would not be molested. This time, Williams was dressed in a large overcoat that changed his appearance. Once at the house, Williams refused to talk to or look directly at Verna until forced to do so. This time, she positively identified him as the man who had entered the house, struck her grandfather and tried to assault her. Deputy Root arrested Williams. Fearing the return to the village, Williams asked the officers to drive him to Avon in Livingston County, which they did. Williams was then locked up in the Avon Jail until the next morning, when Sheriff C.C. Halsted arrived to take charge of Williams and transfer him to Geneseo to the county jail.

Upon his arrival at the county jail in Geneseo, Williams broke down and made a partial confession. During the preliminary examination on Monday morning conducted by District Attorney Cook, Williams stated that he was born in Hagerstown, Maryland, and was twenty-one years of age. With the exception of a few years, he was employed in oyster dredging. Most of his life had been spent as a longshoreman. He also claimed that for three years he had been employed as a stable boy for Mr. James Gordon Bennet, going with him to Paris and London. Since leaving Mr. Bennet's farm, his main occupation was roaming about the country and drinking.

Williams said that he came to Honeoye Falls and was staying at the home of Jesse Hall. On the Saturday morning of the crime, he shoveled snow from a church walk, and with the money, he bought five drinks of gin. Later in the day, he said he fell in with another black man, who gave him two hits of cocaine. He vaguely recalled going to a house after crossing a bridge and engaging in a fight with a man and a woman and hitting them with a club. He had no memory of any incident with the girl, Verna.

There were so many stories circulating around the towns and village that the *Rochester Union and Advertiser* sent a reporter to interview Jesse Hall. Mr. Hall talked freely and expressed sorrow when speaking of James Duffy. According to Hall, Williams had come to Honeoye Falls two years before and worked for C.R. Barnard and, later, Matt Seymour, who lived on a farm adjoining Mr. Duffy's place. It was probably then that Williams met the Duffy family. Since then, according to Hall, Williams claimed that he had been in New York, had pneumonia, had come to Rochester after his recovery and, in Rochester, had been given a ticket by the Salvation Army to come to Honeoye Falls. Mr. Hall took pity on him and took him in, doctoring him until he was able to work again. Hall was a friend of James Duffy and could not understand how Williams could have done such a despicable deed.

On Thursday, February 23, while James Williams was in the county jail in Geneseo, the funeral for James Duffy was held. He was buried in West Bloomfield Rural Cemetery next to his wife. According to his obituary, Duffy was born in Ossining, New York, and had been a resident of the Honeoye Falls community for twenty-eight years. He was a veteran of the Civil War

Gravestone of James Duffy, West Bloomfield, New York Rural Cemetery. *Author's collection.*

and had served with the Old Thirteenth Regiment from April 1861 to May 1863. He had been wounded at the first Battle of Bull Run but had finished his term and was honorably discharged. He was married to Miss Ellen Mann of Pittsford, who predeceased him, in July 1864. He left behind four sons and three daughters.

James Williams was charged with first-degree murder. His trial began on Monday, June 8, 1912. It was held in the Supreme Court in Geneseo, New York. Judge Benton presided. District Attorney Frank S. Cook and Assistant District Attorney Fred A. Quirk presented the case for the prosecution, and Attorneys Charles D. Newton and William Flynn represented the defendant, James Williams. The trial lasted four days.

The case for the prosecution was short and direct. Williams had made a partial confession prior to the trial. Verna Duffy had positively identified Williams as the man who struck her grandfather and aunt and then assaulted her. There was no doubt that James Williams was guilty. The question was: was he guilty of first-degree murder, or were there mitigating circumstances?

The defense needed to try to prove that Williams was not guilty of murder because he was insane at the time, and his insanity was due to epileptic seizures. Sheriff Wilcox and the prison guards had witnessed seizures almost daily while Williams was in jail. Williams's attorney, Flynn, was present at seven different times when Williams had "fits." In describing the fits, Attorney Flynn said that Williams appeared to imagine that he was fighting and would cry out that a mob was after him. Trying to escape the mob, he would hide under his cot in his cell. Sometimes Williams would seize an imaginary person and exclaim, "Aha, now I've got you!" and go through the motions of choking him as if he were an enemy. Much of the time, Attorney Flynn said, when Williams was suffering from these fits he would simply lie on his cot, groan and toss about and, when spoken to, could not recognize anyone. At other times, Williams acted peaceful and thought he was milking cows or herding sheep. All of this was brought out in the defense case and was corroborated by a fellow prisoner.

In 1911, epilepsy was not as well understood as it is today. Apparently, this court had never had a case before it where a person pleaded not guilty on account of epilepsy because the court (not the prosecution or defense) called in several doctors who were considered to be experts on "conditions of the mind and nerves" to testify. Dr. Frederick Sexton of Rochester, who had made a special study of diseases of the mind and nerves, testified that he had made three different examinations of Williams. From the description of the seizures Williams had, Dr. Sexton was unable to give an opinion about whether it was truly epilepsy. He said, however, that Williams's initial crying, falling to the floor and unconsciousness were signs of epilepsy, but he cautioned that they were not all the signs. Dr. Sexton was asked by the prosecution about the inability of Williams to recall completely the events surrounding his attack on Duffy and his family. Dr. Sexton replied that he had not come to any definite conclusions but that it might be a form of epilepsy. He said it wasn't uncommon for someone having this physical form of epilepsy to have recollection problems. "However," said Dr. Sexton, "from all the facts which I have found in my examination of Williams and those I have been given, they are sufficient for me to conclude that he is defective."

The description of "defective" is difficult to define. It could mean that Williams was an epileptic, since in the early 1900s that would have been looked on as a defect, or it could mean that he had a low IQ—or both. Dr. Frederick Merriman, also a nerve and mind specialist from Rochester, testified that he had assisted Dr. Sexton in the examination of Williams. He stated that Williams was able to count to twenty in his presence but could only count to nine in court. He, too, was unable to determine whether the seizures that Williams had were epileptic or not. They contained some of the usual features of epilepsy, but these could have other causes as well. He did state that Williams's moral conception was on a par with his physical constitution, and they were both far below average.

To counter the testimony concerning epilepsy and the insinuation that Williams was insane as a result, District Attorney Cook called several farmers for whom Williams had worked to testify. Not one of them could remember Williams ever having fits. Next, Cook called Jesse Hall and his wife to testify. Williams had stayed with the Halls when he was in Honeoye Falls. Neither of them could remember Williams having fits, and they testified that, in their opinion, Williams appeared mentally sound.

As a last resort, the defense called James Williams, the defendant, to the stand. He repeated the story of his actions of the day of the crime, how he had shoveled snow and drunk some gin. He said that Quintus Lewis had given him some dope and that his senses left him early in the evening; an hour or two later, he had found himself in an alley. He said he faintly remembered having a fight with someone. He could not remember anything specific, and much of what he could remember was a blur.

After a weeklong trial, the jury got the case on Saturday afternoon. The deliberation took only an hour. When asked if they had agreed on a verdict, foreman G.H. Foster of the Town of Groveland announced that they had found Williams guilty of first-degree murder as charged in the indictment. Throughout the trial, Williams had appeared unconcerned about what was happening or being said. When the verdict was read, he wilted a little but seemed to grit his teeth and stepped steadily up to the clerk of the court when asked questions about his birth, degree of education and other crimes. To these questions, he replied that he was twenty-one years old, a resident of New York City, a farm laborer with no education, a Roman Catholic and both his parents were dead. When asked if he had anything to say about why the sentence should not be pronounced, he seemed not to understand and did not reply. Judge Benton explained that the law fixed the sentence regarding first-degree murder and that it was his duty to fix the time for carrying it out. The sentence of the court was that Williams be taken to Auburn Prison and remain there until the week of July 17, when he would be electrocuted. At this point, Williams asked the court if he could be permitted to speak. The court granted his request, and Williams stated that he did not kill Duffy. Judge Benton told him that he had already told that to the jury and it did not believe him.

At this point, one expects that Williams was taken into custody and returned to the county jail to await transfer to Auburn Prison and his execution. That did happen, but not before the unexpected occurred. When Williams heard Judge Benton tell him that the jury did not believe him, he threw up his arms and, from his left sleeve, whipped out a razor blade. With a movement "quicker than a flash," he drew it across his throat. He fell at the feet of Verna Duffy, the girl he had assaulted and the principle witness

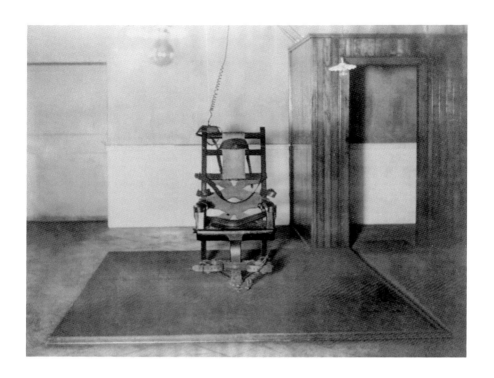

against him. She screamed. The other women in the court began screaming; some fainted, and others hurried to leave the room.

Three deputies caught Williams as he fell. He was struggling so much that they could barely hold on to him. They finally got him under control and back to his cell. No one could explain how Williams managed to conceal the razor blade. It had been known for weeks that a razor blade had been lost in the jail. Williams's person had been searched three times, and his cell had been thoroughly searched for the blade.

James Williams was eventually transferred to Auburn Prison to await his execution. It was reported that he met with his religious counselor, Father A.A. Hughes, while he was incarcerated. Williams reportedly was unconcerned and more rational than during his trial.

Though scheduled for July 17, 1912, Williams's sentence was not carried out until September 16, 1912.

On June 14, 1888, Governor David B. Hill had signed legislation establishing electrocution as the method of executing death sentences for crimes committed after January 1, 1889. Electrocutions using the electric chair were to take place in the three New York State prisons: Auburn, Clinton and Sing Sing. The condemned person was to be held in solitary confinement until his execution. After an autopsy, he would be buried in quicklime in the prison cemetery if relatives did not claim the body. Since Williams's parents were dead and there seemed to be no relatives, we assume that he was buried in Auburn Prison Cemetery.

There is an interesting observation pertaining to this case. It has to do with the question of epilepsy. It seems more likely that Williams did not suffer from epilepsy but from a combination of alcohol and drug abuse. He admitted that before coming to Honeoye Falls, he had wandered around, mostly drinking, and that on the day of the crime he had been drinking gin and had been using cocaine. What appeared to be fits back in 1911 were more likely symptoms of withdrawal, since the fits seemed to lessen with time. The cocaine would also account for his inability to remember the details of the crime. This does not make him "not guilty" of killing Mr. Duffy, but it might have reduced the charge enough to have spared him the electric chair.

Opposite, top: An electric chair in the Auburn Prison, Auburn, New York. *Courtesy of Todd Allen, Monroe County Sheriff's Office.*

Opposite, bottom: Gravestone of Verna Duffy Pestel, West Bloomfield Rural Cemetery. Pestel died in 1990 and was accosted by James Williams in 1911. *Author's collection.*

The last comment on the case belongs to the *Honeoye Falls Times* of June 8, 1911. The *Times* wrote, "Curious as it all is, it seems a singular fate that a man like James Duffy, himself a veteran of the Civil War, should help free a race from slavery when after a lifetime spent in the acts of peace should meet his own end at the hands of one of the race he helped free."

Verna Duffy, the granddaughter of James Duffy, married Leigh Pestel, who served in World War I and died in 1959. Verna died in 1990 at the age of ninety-seven—totally recovered from her struggle with James Williams. Verna and Leigh were both buried in the West Bloomfield Rural Cemetery.

12

Dead Under the Tree

Murder of William Smith, July 12, 1912

The headlines in the *Honeoye Falls Times* read, "Farm Hand Thought to Have Been Murdered, William Smith Found with Crushed Skull— Three Held by Coroner." The man, William Smith, was more commonly known as "Toad." He was forty-four years old. He had been employed and was living in Rochester, but now he was lying under a tree in the Town of Mendon, dead. Thomas Morrisey of Mendon and George Clark were under arrest, and James Maher of Victor was being held as a witness.

The remains of William Smith were taken to the E.G. Brooks Undertaking Room in the Village of Honeoye Falls. Dr. Benjamin White, under the direction of Coroner Kleindiest, performed an autopsy. He found evidence that Smith had been beaten. There were two wounds on the head, a horizontal cut an inch long over the left eye, two bruises a little over an inch in length on the head behind the left cheek and a depression behind the right ear. There were cuts and bruises on both arms. Dr. White concluded that Smith had been beaten and struck on the head. The strike on the head caused a concussion and considerable bleeding and resulted in cerebral hemorrhage and death. Since it was Morrisey who had found Smith under the tree, and since Smith was last seen in the company of Thomas Morrisey and George Clark and there was the accusation that considerable drinking had been going on, the coroner's verdict was simple: "I find that Smith had several contused wounds on his head. They were received at some time during the night of July 11 and that he was left lying at the side of the highway, under a tree, all night in an unconscious condition. I find that said injuries were inflicted by one Thomas

Morrisey and one George Clark, or both, as both persons are under arrest. I hold them responsible for the death of William Smith."

So how did Smith, a laborer living in Rochester, come into the company of Morrisey and Clark and end up dead? Apparently, Morrisey, who owned a farm in Mendon, hired Smith and Clark to cut hay. On Monday morning, Mrs. Morrisey said that her husband left the farm with Smith and Clark. They were going to cut hay on a piece of land that Morrisey owned about a half mile from his farm. She claimed that when her husband returned to the house on Thursday night, only Clark was with him. She said that both had been drinking, but she claimed they were not drunk. They left the next morning, Friday, to go to another farm, she said.

Mr. Betram Gibson of East Mendon was a farmer and a horse trader. He went to see Morrisey on that Thursday morning to buy some oats. He met Morrisey, Clark and Smith at the Wangman Hotel. They were there until noon. Clark and Smith, according to Gibson, left the hotel before him and Morrisey, apparently intending to walk to the farm. Gibson and Morrisey left later and drove to the farm. When Gibson and Morrisey got to the farm, they found Smith and Clark in a scuffle. The two had quarreled over horses. They were in the road, and Clark had thrown Smith to the ground. Morrisey told them to stop, and they did. Gibson acknowledged that all of them had been drinking.

The owner of the Wangman Hotel, Charles Wangman, also verified that the men, Morrisey, Clark and Smith, all had been drinking that Thursday morning. He also claimed that they were not drunk when they left, and he did not hear, see or have any trouble with the men.

It seems, then, from the information given from those who had contact with Morrisey, Clark and Smith, that on Thursday morning, the three of them had been drinking. They made it to the farm, where the next morning Smith was found under a tree, dead. Two of the men, Smith and Clark, had a fight in which Smith was knocked down. On Thursday night, only Morrisey and Clark returned to Morrisey's home. None of the people who were questioned in the investigation into Smith's death said that Morrisey or Clark were drunk.

Thomas Morrisey found Smith unconscious under the tree on Friday morning. He said he went to Mendon to get stimulants, but when he returned, he found Smith dead. He was the one who reported the death. He said nothing about leaving Smith there the night before.

When Sheriff Hamill and Coroner Kleindiest arrived and began an investigation into Smith's death, they found witnesses who saw Smith being pulled along the ground. His injuries indicated that he had been in a brawl, perhaps a drunken brawl. When Morrisey and Clark were brought before Justice of the Peace Furlong on Friday, they were intoxicated, and Clark had a badly swollen hand as if he had been in a fight. The sheriff also took a third man into custody along with Morrisey and Clark. He was James Maher, an older man from Victor, who presumably was a witness to what happened to Smith.

Morrisey, Clark and Maher were taken to the Monroe County Jail to await a grand jury hearing on the case. Morrisey was able to make the bail of $1,000 and released. The grand jury apparently did not believe that there was enough evidence to indict either Clark or Morrisey for manslaughter. Clark was released, and Morrisey's bail was returned.

The murder of William Smith, the man found under the tree in Mendon, has never been solved.

13

"I Thought She Was Dead"

The Abduction and Assault of Elizabeth Sibley Gonzales,
February 28, 1944

Every town has its notable individuals. Here in the Town of Mendon, the Sibleys are one such notable family. Colonel Sibley built a sawmill in the Sibleyville area in the 1830s on Honeoye Creek. His son, Hiram, built a mill and later moved the business to the city of Rochester, but the family continued to own several acres of land in Mendon on what became known as Sibley Road in the area known as Sibleyville. By the 1900s, the home on Sibley Road was used as a weekend and/or vacation home by Harper Sibley and his family while they maintained a residence in the city, where the family was equally as well known. The abduction and assault of a Sibley daughter was big news not only here in Mendon but also throughout all of Monroe County.

Elizabeth Sibley Gonzalez was the twenty-seven-year-old daughter of Harper Sibley, former president of the United States Chamber of Commerce and former national president of the United Service Organizations. She was a graduate of the Masters School in Dobbs Ferry, New York, and had been active in the Junior League in Rochester. She was married to a Stanford University and Harvard Law School graduate, Michael Gonzalez, who was now a lieutenant in the navy. At the time of her abduction, she was working in the training department of the Eastman Kodak Company, where she had enrolled for a wartime job.

On the morning of February 28, 1944, she was driving to work. She stopped for a signal light at the intersection of Alexander Street and East

Hiram Sibley House, 400 East Avenue, Rochester, New York. *Author's collection.*

Avenue when two young men standing on the curb asked her for a ride. Before she could put the car in gear and drive away, they stepped from the curb, opened the rear door of her car and jumped in. At the next corner, one of the men jammed a gun against Mrs. Gonzalez's back and directed her to turn onto Charlotte Street, warning her not to cry out and at the same time assuring her that "we only want the car." They then ordered Mrs. Gonzalez to pull over to the curb and stop. "Al, you get over and drive," said one of the men. Al took the wheel, and the other man remained in the back seat and continued to hold the gun on Mrs. Gonzalez.

The two captors drove around the city of Rochester, seemingly unable to decide where to go or what to do. Along the way, they asked Mrs. Gonzalez if she had any money and asked for her jewelry. She told them, "I'm only carrying a little change in my pocket." They took that, as well as the yellow-gold ring, mounted with emeralds and diamonds, that she was wearing on her ungloved right hand. They were unaware of the valuable engagement ring she wore on her left gloved hand. All the while driving around, they continued to threaten Mrs. Gonzalez and repeat their demands for money and jewelry.

Eventually, they turned south, going out of the city, and as fate would have it, they ended up in the Sibleyville area of the Town of Mendon, where they noticed a deserted half-burned farmhouse. After circling around it, they finally pulled up in front. As it turned out, the farmhouse was only a short distance from the borders of the Sibley family estate, which was owned by Mrs. Gonzalez's father.

The two captors ordered Mrs. Gonzalez out of the car and into the basement of the ruined farmhouse. She was forced to walk through several inches of water and debris to a point up against a far wall. Al's companion then said, "Go ahead, Al, you know what to do with her." With an automatic pistol in his hand, Al approached Mrs. Gonzalez. Mrs. Gonzalez knew that Al was going to kill her. Hoping to stall for time, she asked for her Eastman Kodak employee pass that was still in her car. Al ordered his companion to get the pass. After returning with the pass, Al told his partner to wait in the car. Turning to Mrs. Gonzalez, Al told her, "You won't need this today."

"What are you going to do?" asked Mrs. Gonzalez.

"I'm going to kill you," replied Al.

Faced with death and knowing the odds were against her, Mrs. Gonzalez threw herself at the armed man, taking him by surprise. She succeeded in wresting the weapon from his hand. She turned the weapon on the gunman and pulled the trigger—but nothing happened. For whatever reason, the gun did not fire. Perhaps it was unloaded, but more likely, the safety mechanism was still in place, preventing it from firing. Al then picked up a broken chair rung and struck Mrs. Gonzalez, knocking her unconscious. By the time she regained consciousness, the two men had gone, taking her car with them.

Half dazed and bleeding, Mrs. Gonzalez made her way out of the farmhouse ruins and walked about a quarter of a mile down the road to the farmhouse of Edward Elias. When Elias saw her and heard her story, he immediately notified the sheriff. Chief Deputy O'Laughlin and Deputies Mosher and Flynn quickly went to the scene. In spite of her condition, Mrs. Gonzalez was able to provide the officers with a detailed description of her captors before she was taken by ambulance to the hospital in Rochester. Word was also sent to the Rochester Detective Bureau, where Chief Collins ordered an eight-state Teletype alert with descriptions of the two men and the missing car, including its license plate, MR-43.

At the abandoned farmhouse where Mrs. Gonzalez was held, the deputies found her Kodak pass and one of her gloves, which had apparently been dropped in the struggle. They also found parts of a broken chair that were determined to be the parts of the chair used to strike Mrs. Gonzalez. On further examination of the chair parts, it was determined that Mrs. Gonzalez had been struck not once but several times after she was knocked down.

Elizabeth Sibley Gonzalez (inset) and the scene of her assault in Sibleyville, Town of Mendon. *From the* Rochester Democrat & Chronicle, *February 29, 1944.*

On the morning following her abduction, Mrs. Gonzalez was asked to look through several hundred mug shots of known felons. She was able to pick out two pictures, declaring definitively that they were the men who had abducted her. With these pictures and descriptions in hand, all members of the Detective Bureau, the sheriff's office and the local area state police were put on twenty-four-hour duty to apprehend the wanted men.

Simultaneously, District Attorney Daniel J. O'Mara, using Mrs. Gonzalez's recollection that one of the men had been called Al by his companion, searched through his criminal indictment files. He came up with an automobile theft indictment against an Albert Stuckrath. Another detective, Joseph Haggerty, who had picked up Stuckrath in Florida when he was arrested on a former indictment, recalled that Stuckrath had a close friend named Thomas Pampalone. This information was promptly turned over to Chief Collins. With this knowledge, police started questioning friends of Stuckrath and Pampalone. One informant told police that he had heard that the men were staying in the Manhattan Street area, so police were immediately sent into the area, and a house-to-house canvass began.

On a routine check of Stuckrath's and Pampalone's families, Assistant Detective Chief Lambiase and Detectives Foubister and Daily went to the home of Pampalone's sister. To their amazement, Pampalone himself answered the door. He was immediately arrested and taken to police headquarters. At first, he refused to tell them where he and Stuckrath had been staying, but after further questioning, he finally admitted to his part in the abduction and robbery of Mrs. Gonzalez.

Later in the afternoon of the same day, Deputy Sheriffs Mosher and Flynn were cruising on Monroe Avenue, a main street in the city, when they saw a man answering Stuckrath's description walking down the avenue. Deputy Flynn drove up alongside him, and Deputy Mosher jumped out. Stuckrath made an attempt to run around the end of the deputy's car but was not quick enough and was captured.

The close cooperation among the Rochester Police Department, the sheriff's office and the local state police had resulted in the swift apprehension of both Stuckrath and Pampalone within four days of committing the crime.

Under questioning, the two suspects recounted their activities in the days between committing of the crime and their capture. They said that after leaving Mrs. Gonzalez in the farmhouse, they drove back to Rochester. They abandoned her car in the northwest section of the city sometime after 10:00 a.m. that day. They carefully wiped the car clean of any fingerprints and tossed Mrs. Gonzalez's handbag on a city trash collection truck. Then they parted company.

Pampalone went to work at a downtown store, where he was employed as a clerk. Stuckrath went home, changed his clothes and began to make a series of phone calls to the district attorney's office and police headquarters.

Stuckrath, at the time of Mrs. Gonzalez's abduction, was out on bail. He had been arrested back on February 19 and charged with second-degree larceny for the theft of an automobile belonging to Sylvester Osburn of Greece, New York, five days earlier. He had been released on $1,000 bail, which had been guaranteed by a property bond from his parents. As part of his bail, he was required to report to the district attorney's office at 10:20 a.m. on Monday. He arrived late and was subsequently sent to the city court at police headquarters to arrange another adjournment of his case. He told Deputy Lambiase and District Attorney O'Mara that he had placed the .32-caliber automatic pistol he used in the abduction of Mrs. Gonzalez in his outside coat pocket with the safety catch off. He said that he was prepared to shoot anyone who attempted to arrest him for what he thought at the time was the murder of Mrs. Gonzalez. As luck would have it, he was not recognized as the suspect in the Gonzalez case, and his stolen car case was adjourned until March 16. He had simply walked out of police headquarters.

Later that same day, Stuckrath said, after he saw the first newspaper account of the kidnapping and bludgeoning of Mrs. Gonzalez, he visited Pampalone at the Main Street store where he worked to discuss a plan to avoid arrest and to escape. Later that afternoon, he returned to the store and told Pampalone that he had rented an apartment where they could hide out.

Stuckrath and Pampalone were arraigned in Rochester City Court and charged with first-degree robbery, first-degree grand larceny and first-degree kidnapping. These alleged crimes were all committed within the city limits. Next, the two men were taken to the Town of Mendon and arraigned before Justice Livermore. Here, they were both charged with first-degree assault for the beating of Mrs. Gonzalez in the abandoned farmhouse. Even though, according to Stuckrath's confession, Pampalone did not take part in the beating, nor was he even present when it occurred, he also faced the first-degree assault charge as he was engaged in the commission of a crime when and at the time the beating took place.

Following their questioning, both Stuckrath and Pampalone were taken to Genesee Hospital, where they both identified Mrs. Gonzalez as the woman they had kidnapped and robbed. She in turn identified them positively as the two men who held her up.

"Not only did their confessions bear out in every detail to Mrs. Gonzalez's account of her abduction, robbery and beating in a deserted, half-burned farmhouse near the estate of her father at Sibleyville, but it also developed that one of the men had intended to kill her and believed he had when he left the farmhouse," Assistant Detective Chief Lambiase said. Lambiase asked Stuckrath, "If you hadn't been satisfied that she was dead, would you have shot her?"

"Yes. I would," Stuckrath replied.

The case was presented to the Monroe County Grand Jury by District Attorney Daniel O'Mara. He summoned eleven witnesses, but his most convincing witness was Mrs. Gonzalez, who was accompanied by her husband, Lieutenant Michael Gonzalez, on leave from his naval duties in Panama, and her father, the well-known Harper Sibley. After hearing the testimony, the grand jury handed down a seven-count indictment accusing Stuckrath and Pampalone of kidnapping, first-degree robbery, first-degree assault and first-degree grand larceny. The specific indictment contained one count charging the "seized, confined, inveigled and kidnapped" Mrs. Gonzalez; four counts of robbery for taking the ring and cash; one count of

Albert Stuckrath and Thomas Pampalone, abductors of Elizabeth Sibley Gonzalez. *From the Rochester Democrat & Chronicle, March 3, 1944.*

assault for attacking her with the chair rungs, cited as a "means and force likely to produce death"; and one count of grand larceny for auto theft. Stuckrath also had been indicted the week before on second-degree grand theft of an automobile two weeks before the abduction of Mrs. Gonzalez.

Pampalone and Stuckrath, who were both eighteen years of age, made full confessions. For pleading guilty in the kidnap, robbery and beating of Mrs. Elizabeth Sibley Gonzalez, they were both sentenced to long terms in Attica Prison. Pampalone was sentenced to fifteen to thirty years on the robbery count and five to ten years on the assault count. Both terms would run consecutively.

Before he was sentenced, Stuckrath admitted that he had been convicted of auto theft in 1942 and had served a term in West Coxsakie State Prison. Because of this previous conviction, Judge O'Connor sentenced Stuckrath to a longer sentence. Describing the crimes as "most vicious and atrocious," Judge O'Connor said to Stuckrath, "Stuckrath, your unwarranted and cowardly assault on this defenseless woman cannot be excused. The fact that she wasn't killed isn't any fault of yours. You thought she was killed and so stated. I feel that your assault shows a depraved mind, a viciously depraved mind, and that you are not worthy of the permission to associate with decent people. You are not worthy to have the liberties of decent people." He then sentenced Stuckrath to twenty to forty years on the robbery count and ten to twenty years on the assault charge, both to be served consecutively.

The attorneys for the convicted men, Reuben Brodsky and Philip Scardino, pleaded with Judge O'Connor to have the sentences run concurrently rather than consecutively. Scardino told the court that Pampalone was suffering from an active case of tuberculosis. Judge O'Connor refused their request and expressed the belief that Pampalone would receive better treatment in an institution than he might get otherwise. "I have given a good deal of consideration to these cases, and I don't feel that the sentences are too harsh," the judge told the lawyers. "As far as Stuckrath's sentence, I think it is lenient rather than harsh."

Pampalone and Stuckrath were transferred to Attica Prison to serve their sentences. According to the District Attorney's Office, Stuckrath would become eligible for parole when he reached thirty-eight years of age, or sometime in 1964. Pampalone would be eligible for parole at age thirty-four if he survived.

Unfortunately, it appears that Thomas Pampalone did not survive very long. A check of cemetery records turned up a Thomas Pampalone, who died and was buried in Holy Sepulchre Cemetery in Rochester on April 26, 1947, at the age of twenty-two. This corresponds with the age of the convicted Thomas Pampalone.

A search for Albert Stuckrath turned up an article in a Jacksonville, Florida newspaper (date unknown) about an Albert Stuckrath who had been given thirty to sixty years in prison for a robbery and assault in Rochester, New York. A search of the Social Security Death Index turned up an Albert W. Stuckrath, who was born on October 25, 1925, in New York and died on April 24, 2006, at age eighty-one. His last residence was listed as Jesup, Wayne County, Georgia.

In an interview, after the capture of Stuckrath and Pampalone, Police Chief Henry Copenhagen, Detective Chief Edward Collins, Sheriff Albert Skinner and Lieutenant Charles LaForge of the state police all agreed that credit for solving the case belonged to Mrs. Gonzalez—her coolness while in "peril," which enabled her to note various characteristics of her kidnapers; her ability to give investigators such minute descriptions of her kidnapers' personal appearances and physical characteristics that police labeled them the most perfect they had ever received; her ability to select two men without hesitation from among several hundred photographs and to positively identify them as her kidnappers; and her ability to give a clear account of her experiences. Despite the serious beating she underwent, which checked so closely with the reported confessions of the young men arrested that there could be no question of the truth in their stories, the officers were of the opinion that these were the most important factors in solving the case so quickly.

14

Junkyard Murder

Murder of George Burmeister, December 7, 1972

E very town and village has its unusual individuals. Some people might call them characters; others might call them eccentric or a nuisance, and still others simply shake their heads and try to ignore them. The Village of Honeoye Falls and the Town of Mendon had such a character. His name was George Burmeister.

The Burmeister family owned thirty-six acres of land on Amann Road in the Town of Mendon. They were the type of people who never threw anything away. By the time son George returned home in 1966 from Pennsylvania at the age of thirty-six, the house was so full of "stuff" that no one other than the family could enter the home. Upon his return, George operated a private garbage collection business, and the junk in and around the house increased. It was suggested that for George, collecting junk was as much a business as it was a hobby.

Customers often came to the property looking for salvaged automobile parts. A neighbor commented, "He didn't sell much." Kids from the area around Mendon and Honeoye Falls would often go to Burmeister looking for an old carburetor or muffler. Some of his biggest items were tires and old inner tubes. He had many kinds of tires. The price for one might be anywhere from "a dime to half a buck."

George Burmeister was a "different" type of man. He never volunteered much information about himself. No one in the area knew anything about where he had been or what he had done prior to his return home. He kept to himself and was often described as a hermit or recluse. He was an intelligent man. Some people described him as brilliant. He was valedictorian of his high school class. He even took college classes at the University of Rochester.

In 1970, his mother died. The local undertaker who removed the body from the Burmeister home was probably the last outsider to have been permitted inside the home. Two years later, when his father died, George carried the corpse out of the house and placed it in one of his junked cars by the side of the road. Then he called the Monroe County Sheriff's Department and said, "My old man died last night. I brought him out in the yard. You come and get him."

When the sheriff's deputies arrived, Burmeister would not let them into the house to use his phone. "You got a two-way radio in your car; use that," he said. The officers used their radio to call the undertaker to remove the body.

No one argued with George Burmeister. He had very definite ideas about "his rights." In 1972, George was on probation as a result of having fired five shots at a state policeman three years before. The state trooper had come to investigate a complaint about one of George's junked automobiles, which was blocking the road. His probation officer, Anthony Annunziata, described George, saying, "I never thought of him as a violent man. Half the time, his reasoning was good. The other half, it wasn't so good. He wasn't the easiest guy to get along with. He felt very strongly about his right to protect his property." When asked about George's junk collection, Annunziata replied, "Maybe it gave him some sense of security."

Aside from junk and privacy, George Burmeister had another love. He loved his animals. He kept at least four cats and a dog named Caesar. No one knew what he actually fed his animals. As for himself, everyone knew that George subsisted on chocolate milk that he bought by the case, Oreo cookies and cornflakes.

George Burmeister died on December 7, 1972, a Thursday, but he was such a private, reclusive man that no one knew he was dead. It was twenty days later, on December 27, when Burmeister's body was found and even longer before his death was declared a homicide.

The first indication that something was wrong at the Burmeister home came from the Rochester Telephone Company. On the afternoon of December 7, the specialized equipment in the telephone company office noted that Burmeister's phone was off the hook. When this occurred, the telephone gave off a steady piercing whine that was loud enough to be heard throughout the house and was picked up by the equipment at the telephone company office. If the whine failed to get a response and was a party line, as was the case with Burmeister, a repairman was sent out within twenty-four hours.

When the repairman arrived at Burmeister's house on December 8, the dog, Caesar, came bounding out from the junk piled between the house and the road, barking furiously. The repairman carefully made his way through the collection of junk and tires to the door. His hammering on the door got no response, so he cut off Burmeister's phone hookup from the rest of the party line. He left a dated note wedged in the door stating that he had called to inspect the phone and found no one home.

About two weeks after the telephone line was cut, the postman, noticing that the mail was overflowing the mailbox, called the Sheriff's Department. The deputy who took the call attempted to reach Burmeister by phone. When he was unable to reach Burmeister, he drove out to the house and, finding no one around, stopped at Sheriff Deputy Emilie Manzler's house. Manzler was Burmeister's closest neighbor. He asked if she knew anything about Burmeister's whereabouts.

Mrs. Manzler had not noticed anything unusual about the house. She told the deputy that he might have gone away without telling anyone. "I've been noticing the light," she said. Apparently, he always left his doors securely locked and a light on in his bedroom. She also told the deputy that when Burmeister did leave, he always made arrangements for someone to come and feed his old dog, Caesar, but she had noticed that "it looks to me like that dog of his is starving."

On December 27, the telephone repairman made a second visit to the Burmeister home and again found no one there. This time, he reported the matter to Sheriff's Chief Deputy Michael Ceretto.

Chief Deputy Ceretto knew that when Burmeister had been arrested for shooting at a state trooper, he had been represented by a local lawyer. Chief Deputy Ceretto decided to contact the lawyer in order to get permission to enter Burmeister's house. Having received that permission, on Wednesday morning, December 27, Ceretto, along with a party of deputies including Burmeister's neighbor, Emilie Manzler, made their way through the snow-covered, junk-littered yard to the house.

The house had three doors. Two of them were completely blocked by piles of car parts and old furniture. One door, the kitchen door, was not blocked but was locked from the inside. No one responded to their knocks or shouts, so this locked door was the first indication that something was wrong.

The deputies picked the lock on the door, but in spite of ramming it with their shoulders and kicking at the wood below the knob, they were unable to force it open. One of the deputies, Sergeant William Abigail, stripped off a patch of lath and looked through a crack in the paneling. All that could be seen was a narrow path between piles of old newspapers and magazines and something that looked like a dirty brown duffle bag propped against the base of the kitchen door. They were also able to see two scrawny cats, one black and one white, crouched on a pile of rags and staring at the door. A second look at what appeared to be a duffle bag had the deputies wondering if it actually was a bag or something else.

Finally, the deputies were able to force open a kitchen window and hack their way through the piles of papers and junk to the path between the newspapers they had seen from the door. What looked like a dirty duffle bag turned out to be the decomposing remains of George Burmeister, who was slumped against the kitchen door. He had been dead for some time, and tightly clutched in his hand was his telephone. Taking into consideration that the house was locked, Burmeister lived alone and he had a telephone clutched in his hand, the initial thought was that Burmeister died in a futile attempt to summon help.

While waiting for the county identification supervisor, Anthony Yarzback, and the medical examiner, Dr. John Edland, the deputies looked around the house for any evidence of a crime. They found that some of the rooms were heaped so high with litter and junk that there was no way to get into them. To get to Burmeister's bedroom, the deputies were forced to walk sideways through a narrow path between broken furniture, old appliances, crates, battery cases and television sets—one at a time. In the bedroom, they did not find any evidence of a crime—only a mattress covered with a dirty blanket with holes in it that had apparently been chewed by rats.

It was not until the remains of Burmeister had been stripped of its many layers of filthy clothing and the body washed that the medical examiner found a small-caliber bullet hole in Burmeister's chest. It was confirmed by the autopsy that Burmeister had been shot with a .22-caliber slug, which passed through his heart and lodged in his lung. The medical examiner concluded that Burmeister probably died within a minute after the bullet entered his body.

A canvass of the neighbors determined that December 7 was the last day that Burmeister was seen wandering through the piles of junked cars and sorting through his rubble. Monroe County sheriff Albert Skinner made a public appeal for help. It resulted in a number of potential leads. One such lead was from a truck driver who lived on Boughton Hill Road not too far from Burmeister's property. He recalled seeing a battered white convertible leaving Burmeister's driveway on the afternoon of December 7—the last day anyone saw Burmeister alive.

As luck would have it, Detective Sergeant Donald Clark also remembered having seen a battered white convertible, but not at the Burmeister home. Clark, who had been visiting Ontario County during the second week of December, had taken a look at a battered white Valiant convertible that had been impounded by the Ontario County sheriff. The Valiant had been found abandoned on the Victor–Holcomb Road in Ontario County, which bordered Monroe County. The car was towed from Holcomb to the Monroe County garage, and the sheriff and state police technicians carefully examined it. There was no doubt that the car was a "junker" with lots of problems. The technicians found fingerprints all over the car that were thought to be those of Burmeister and his killer.

At the same time, Chief Deputy Ceretto was checking with youths in the area who at one time or another had purchased car parts form Burmeister. Chief Ceretto learned that often Burmeister would "hire" young men to help out in the junkyard. Instead of cash, Burmeister usually paid the young men in salvaged automobile parts or other usable junk. Chief Deputy Ceretto proceeded to question each of these men.

One of the young men lived in Greece. He was able to satisfactorily account for his whereabouts on the day Burmeister was killed. He also agreed to adopt Caesar, Burmeister's dog. A second youth lived in Mendon Center. He, too, was able to account for his whereabouts and was cleared of suspicion. A third youth, a former Bloomfield High School student, could not be found.

Since the missing young man was thought to be a resident of Holcomb in Ontario County, Sheriff Skinner asked for the assistance of the Ontario County Sheriff's Department. It wasn't long before it became clear to the officers that the missing young man was very likely involved in the Burmeister murder. A tip from a Manchester resident strengthened this conviction. The resident reported that while driving toward Canandaigua, he was flagged down by a young man walking along the road carrying a small rifle. "He was heading east on Route 5," the resident said. "He told me he lived up near the lake and that he'd been hunting rabbits in the woods near Mud Creek. I let him out of the car near the turnoff of Route 2."

With this information, the Ontario County officers notified the Monroe County sheriff that they were on the trail of an eighteen-year-old man named David Paul Crossett. Crossett was a Bloomfield High School dropout. When the officers went to his address, they discovered that he had not lived with his family for some time, and they thought that he was living with friends.

The officers proceeded to the friends' home, where they learned that Crossett had been there that morning but had packed and left shortly after breakfast. The officers examined the belongings that Crossett had left behind but found nothing that would connect him to the murder of Burmeister. Sometime later, they spoke to Crossett's mother. She told them that she saw him bury a gun near her house.

Acting on information supplied by Crossett's friends, the officers went to Oak Manor Apartments off Routes 5 and 20 in Holcomb. When they pulled up, Crossett bolted out of the back door and ran into a wooded area that opened out on a road. By the time Crossett came into the open, officers in another car had cut him off. Crossett was arrested by Sergeant Harry DeHollander, now retired and a resident of Mendon, and taken to the Monroe County Sheriff's Headquarters to be questioned. Crossett did not put up a fight.

At the Monroe County Sheriff's Headquarters, David Paul Crossett made a full and voluntary confession of the murder of George Burmeister. At seven o'clock that same night, December 29, he was arraigned before Mendon town justice Russell C. Matthews. Matthews entered a mandatory plea of innocent for Crossett since he had no attorney. He was then sent to Rochester to be held in jail without bail.

Crossett's statement and confession told of a growing argument between himself and Burmeister over the white Valiant convertible. The argument had begun in late summer. Crossett claimed that Burmeister had given him the old car in partial payment for work he had done for him. When the car broke down, Burmeister told Crossett that he "could take parts from other junkers to fix it." Crossett said he worked on the convertible in Burmeister's yard, but when he finally got it running, Burmeister reneged on the deal and would not let him take the car.

"He said he wouldn't give it to me unless I did more work for him in the junkyard," Crossett said. "I refused, and we began to argue." Crossett said his last attempt to persuade Burmeister to give him the car was around Thanksgiving, the police said. When Burmeister refused again, Crossett decided to take another course of action.

On the afternoon of December 7, neighbors saw George Burmeister working on an old truck in his yard. Finishing with the truck, Burmeister went to his house, entered the kitchen and locked the door behind him. According to Crossett's statement, he had slipped into the house when Burmeister wasn't looking and was waiting for him when he entered the kitchen and locked the door. Crossett said he called out Burmeister's name, "George!" Burmeister, Crossett said, reached for his phone and said, "Hi, kid." At that moment, Crossett raised his rifle, took aim and put a shot into

Burmeister's heart. Burmeister slumped to the floor still clutching the phone in his hand.

After shooting Burmeister, according to Monroe County authorities, Crossett waited a few minutes to see if, in fact, Burmeister was dead. Finally, he crawled with his gun over the piles of junk and trash and climbed out a partly broken window at the side of the house. He started up the Valiant convertible and headed out toward Holcomb. Unfortunately for him, the car stalled, and Crossett was forced to walk carrying his rifle. Thumbing, he was able to get two rides, each time explaining that he had been hunting.

On June 7, 1973, David Paul Crossett went on trial for the murder of George Burmeister. Crossett pleaded guilty to first-degree manslaughter. Judge Edward C. Provanzano sentenced Crossett to up to twenty-five years in Attica Prison. After passing sentence, Provanzano said he had received two letters from Crossett expressing regret over what he had done. The judge also noted that the youth had no previous criminal record. "The fact remains," Provanzano told Crossett, "that a life was taken of a person who had approximately twenty-six more years to live."

Crossett was transported to Attica to serve his sentence. George Burmeister was buried in West Bloomfield Rural Cemetery next to the grave of his parents. His house and junkyard remained intact, at least for a time. Donald Corbett, the lawyer handling Burmeister's estate, said that it would take time

Gravestone of George Burmeister, West Bloomfield Rural Cemetery. *Author's collection.*

before the estate would be settled. The land had to be surveyed and the land and house inventoried in case there were any antiques among the junk. Burmeister had no immediate family, but he did have relatives.

According to Town of Mendon supervisor Squire Kingston, the Town of Mendon had been trying for some time to get the property cleaned up. Burmeister had been scheduled to appear in town court on a charge of violating the junkyard statute before he was murdered. "We had hoped to get it cleared up but only expected to get it to conform to the law requiring a certain kind of fencing and certain hours of operations," said Kingston. "Maybe now it will get cleaned up."

Today, all evidence of Burmeister, the "Junkman," is gone.

15

Railroad Mayhem

August 30, 1909

T he Village of Honeoye Falls owes much of its development to the Lehigh Valley and New York Central Railroads. The original settlers depended on the falls and creek to supply water power to run their mills, but it was the coming of the railroads that allowed those mills to send their products all over the United States and even to Europe. There is no doubt that the railroads brought with them economic development and a chance for travel, but they also brought mayhem in the form of disastrous accidents.

The type of locomotive that struck Harrison Reed, Father Cluney and Lorin Parsons in Honeoye Falls; taken in late 1800s. *Courtesy of Honeoye Falls/Mendon Historical Society.*

The New York Central Railroad

The New York Central Railroad tracks ran almost through the heart of downtown Honeoye Falls. One spur ran into the Enterprise Straw Board Mill that was located off Ontario Street near Honeoye Creek. In July 1902, Harrison Reed, a sixty-year-old resident of Bloomfield, was driving his team of horses down Ontario Street. He was on his way to meet his son and a friend who were rafting on Honeoye Creek. Reed had with him a friend, James Utterbeck of Rochester, who was spending the summer in Bloomfield. His route would take him across the New York Central Crossing on Ontario Street.

At the same time, the eastbound freight was returning from the Enterprise Straw Board Mill. It would cross Ontario Street. The train engineer saw Reed and his team of horses approaching the crossing. He pulled the whistle to signal and at the same time reversed the engines and applied the brakes. One of the brakemen also saw Reed and his team and shouted to Reed to drive on across the tracks ahead of the train.

Reed saw the danger immediately and realized that if he drove on as instructed by the brakeman, it would mean instant death. Instead, he reversed his horses. The engine of the train hit the horses. They were thrown several feet ahead of the train. Reed and his passenger, Utterbeck, were thrown from the wagon. Reed fell between the wagon wheel and the passing train wheels in a space not more than two feet wide. His head barely missed being hit by the train wheels. Utterbeck was also thrown from the wagon but in the opposite direction, away from the train.

Hearing the signal, neighbors ran out and witnessed the accident. They quickly assisted Reed onto the nearby porch of C.H. Fairchild. Dr. Hand also heard the train signal and, realizing there was a problem, ran to the scene and was able to attend to Reed and Utterbeck. Both men were lucky. Both received cuts and bruises, and Utterbeck had a broken wrist. The horses did not fare as well. They were so badly injured that they had to be shot on the spot.

In the aftermath of the accident, the village board complained to the railroad and asked that a crossing guard be installed at the Ontario Street crossing and that the shade trees near the crossing that had obscured the view of the tracks be cut. Unfortunately, nothing was done.

Fourteen years later, in 1916, a similar accident occurred at the West Main Street crossing of the New York Central Railroad. This time, the results were deadly.

On January 28, 1916, Father Cluney, the pastor of St. Paul of the Cross Roman Catholic Church, and his sexton, Bruno Pilo, were on their way to the Catholic cemetery to mark out a grave for Nellie, the daughter of Matthew O'Brien. They were riding in an automobile. Mr. O'Brien was scheduled to ride with them, but he did not meet up with them. He decided to walk to the cemetery. He had just crossed the tracks when the automobile was struck by the train.

The engine hit the car just behind the front seat. Father Cluney was thrown to the side of the road, but Pilo and the automobile were carried more than five hundred feet down the track. When the train finally stopped, everyone thought that Pilo was dead.

Father Cluney had somehow managed to escape death. He received a deep cut on his head that required several stitches. He was badly shaken up but otherwise unhurt.

Meanwhile, the train backed into the Honeoye Falls station. It was discovered that Pilo was not dead but was suffering from a fractured skull and numerous other injuries. Local Drs. White and Marlatte were summoned, and they immediately ordered that Pilo be taken to a hospital in Rochester. A special train was quickly made up, and Pilo was rushed to St. Mary's Hospital in Rochester, a trip that took thirty-five minutes. The ambulance was waiting at the station in Rochester, but all efforts to save the man were futile. Bruno Pilo died of his injuries. His body was taken to the Rochester morgue.

Pilo was only thirty-nine years old when he died. He had been sexton at St. Paul of the Cross Roman Catholic Church for nearly six years. He was originally from Italy. He was survived by a wife and two small children.

Coroner Killip held an inquiry into the death of Bruno Pilo. Herman S. Heckman, engineer of the train, was questioned extensively. He stated that the train was running at approximately eighteen miles an hour when it hit the car at the crossing. A Honeoye Falls ordinance prohibited freight trains from running faster than six miles an hour in the village. When asked why he was traveling faster, Heckman replied, "The way was clear." He also said that the automobile must have been traveling at a greater speed than the train and that's why he didn't see the automobile.

Further examination of Engineer Heckman elicited some disturbing information. When asked by the lawyer who represented Father Cluney whether any engineer had been disciplined for breaking rules such as going faster than the speed limit, Heckman replied with a simple "no." Heckman also stated that he had been running the Rochester branch for thirteen years,

Gravestone of Bruno Pilo, St. Paul of the Cross Cemetery, Honeoye Falls, New York. *Author's collection.*

and he could not recall any occasion when he had ever slowed down to six miles. Questioned further by the lawyer, Heckman said that his superiors were unaware that he had exceeded the six-mile-an-hour limit, and he never reported that he did so.

When asked specifically about the accident, Heckman said that he had shut off power at the crossing and drifted to Main Street when the accident occurred. He said he whistled for the crossing and rang the bell until the crossing was reached. When the locomotive hit the car, he said he did not feel any shock, and the first he knew of the collision was when a body shot across in front of the engine—probably Father Cluney's, thrown from the car. The train traveled for a distance of 523 feet before it finally stopped.

The testimony and results of the inquest in the accident caused great concern in the village and renewed demands for safety measures to be placed at the crossing. Again, that would mean a crossing guard being put there. Unfortunately, nothing was done, and Mrs. Pilo, who was left with two small children, lost her lawsuit against the railroad.

The Lehigh Valley Railroad

The New York Central Railroad was not the only one to come into Honeoye Falls. The second was the Lehigh Valley Railroad. Like the New York Central, there were also concerns about the rate of speed in which the trains entered the village and the lack of safety at the crossings. This lack of concern for safety and the need to keep on schedule were responsible for a tragic accident that occurred at the Main Street crossing.

On August 30, 1904, Lorin Parsons, a man of sixty-seven years, owned a meat market in the village. It was his habit to periodically drive to the neighboring town of Lima to get a supply of beef. It was also common for him to take along little eight-year-old Charlie Woodard, and such was the case on this fateful August day. Lorin Parsons, along with little Charlie, drove his horse-drawn wagon to Lima and picked up a supply of beef. They were both sitting on the wagon seat as they drove back into the village and down Main Street toward the Lehigh Valley crossing.

The Lehigh Valley train was coming into the village from the south, from Hemlock Lake. It was due in at 4:30 p.m., but apparently it was behind schedule because it was running at a high rate of speed, certainly more than the six-mile-per-hour speed limit for the village. The engineer saw Parsons driving toward the crossing. He claimed he blew the whistle a second time to warn him, but the wagon and the man and boy did not pay him any heed. An instant later, the horse crossed the tracks. The engineer applied the emergency brake, but it was too late. The locomotive crashed into the wagon loaded with beef.

Mr. Parsons was thrown to the side of the street against a fence. Charlie, the little boy, was thrown up on the "pilot" of the engine and carried several rods down the track. He fell to the side of the track when the engine came to a stop. The trainman picked up Charlie's unconscious body and tenderly carried him back to the crossing. Blood was dripping from a large wound on his head. One of his legs was broken. It was

New York Central Railroad Crossing, West Main Street, Honeoye Falls, New York. *Courtesy of Honeoye Falls/Mendon Historical Society.*

Gravestone of Charles Woodward, Honeoye Falls Cemetery. *Author's collection.*

thought at that time that his injuries were fatal. He was carried to a nearby house belonging to J.K. Smith, where Dr. Boult tended to him a few minutes after the accident.

A second doctor, Dr. White, was also summoned. He examined Mr. Parsons. Parsons was badly injured. One of his legs was crushed, his head was cut open and his chest was crushed. He was placed aboard the train and taken to the Homeopathic Hospital in Rochester, where he died a few minutes after his arrival.

The wagon that Parsons and the boy were riding in was completely destroyed. Only a few pieces of slivered wood and bent and twisted ironwork remained. The horse had made it across the tracks and was uninjured.

Charlie was transported to City Hospital in Rochester aboard a train later that evening. His injuries were severe, but he had a fighting chance. As of November, Charlie was still in the hospital. The wound on his head was not healing in spite of receiving the best medical treatment available at the time. His badly fractured leg was still an "offensive running sore." He had no memory of the accident and thought that he had taken a bad fall. He remembered that he and Mr. Parsons always "looked both directions for trains." He didn't remember hearing anything.

The child's recovery was slow, and he required constant care and attention. The wounds on his head and leg needed daily dressing. This task was so serious that the services of a surgeon were required on each occasion. During his entire recovery, the railroad officials made no inquiry in regard to the boy's condition. They offered no settlement to the boy's family, in spite of the allegations that the train was running at a speed that exceeded the speed set by the village ordinance. The village complained to the railroad, and Charlie Woodard's father started a lawsuit against the Lehigh Valley Railroad.

It is safe to surmise that, at least for a time, trains probably slowed when entering the village. The outcome of Mr. Woodard's lawsuit is unknown. Charlie did eventually recover and lived to be sixty years of age, dying in 1956. He is buried in the Honeoye Falls Cemetery with his wife.

16

Miscellaneous Mayhem

Things happen. Sometimes these happenings are good, sometimes they are bad and sometimes they are funny. This can also be said of mayhem.

DISASTER IN A HAND BASKET

In July 1913, the Village of Honeoye Falls contracted with several men to put in a waterworks. This was no easy task as the village is built on limestone, and you "can't take a shovel to limestone." It requires much more power— dynamite power.

John Evarett was only thirty-eight years old. He was hired to work on the water lines. His job was to use dynamite to blast through the limestone. On the morning of July 24, 1913, John was on his way to work. He was carrying a basket with the tools of his trade—twelve sticks of dynamite and some dry electric batteries, but no blasting caps, at least as far as anyone knew.

On his way to the ditch on Monroe Street, the site of the blasting, he met the contractor on the job, Burt Warren. They had a short conversation. Warren turned one way to the front of the wagon shed, and Evarett turned into the roadway leading to the excavation for the pump house directly in back of the shed. Suddenly, there was an explosion.

The explosion was so loud that people came running from their homes and businesses. The blast broke every window in the nearby warehouse.

The large window in the Lehigh Valley Railway station was blown out. The section of the shed where the explosion occurred was literally reduced to kindling wood. Part of the rear wall of another section of the shed hurtled past Burt Warren's head, missing him by inches. It blew his hat off and knocked him to the ground. There was a hole in the ground where Evarett had been standing.

Evarett was literally blown to pieces by the force of the explosion. His remains were blown a good twenty-five feet from the front of the shed. One of his hands was blown against the side of a nearby warehouse owned by Mr. Jobes. It was found high above the ground at least seventy-five feet from the spot where the explosion occurred, and it traveled with such force that it shattered a hole through the boards. Other fragments of flesh were blown against the warehouse outer wall. Evarett's blood stained the red-painted boards of the warehouse a darker shade. His hands and feet were missing, but later his hands were found by searchers. His body was mangled, and the back of Evarett's head was blown away. Oddly, his face was practically uninjured. Evarett's charred clothing was found in a pile of shed debris, although his remains were blown beyond the shed wreckage.

Immediately after the explosion, workmen and neighbors engaged in the gruesome work of searching for portions of John Evarett. Many other workmen, along with Burt Warren, were so shocked by what happened that they couldn't resume work.

Coroner physician Dr. Boult viewed Evarett's remains. He questioned a number of people, hoping to find an eyewitness to the event. Unfortunately, he was unable to find out exactly what happened as Evarett left the contractor, Burt Warren, and walked to the shed and his death. Dr. Boult called in his findings to the coroner in Rochester and then gave orders for Evarett's remains to be taken to Brook's Undertaking Rooms, where they were prepared for burial.

Burt Warren, who narrowly escaped death or injury, felt terrible about the tragic affair. His hopes of completing the waterworks project without serious injury or death were "dashed."

Good-natured, unassuming John Evarett was survived by a wife and two children. Unfortunately, less than a year later, Mrs. Evarett also died. Both she and her husband are buried in Honeoye Falls Cemetery in unmarked graves.

The last word on the subject belongs to the *Honeoye Falls Times*, which reported that "dynamite is dangerous stuff to handle even in the most careful manner. There are many instances where dynamite has exploded without apparent cause while on other occasions will not cause an explosion."

"Hunting Germans"

Though this last act is in some ways tragic, it contains an element of lightheartedness. It was 1917, and the United States was engaged in the First World War. Our principal enemy was Germany. The front pages of all local papers, such as the *Honeoye Falls Times*, were full of stories and comments on the war.

Frank Potter lived on Monroe Street in the Village of Honeoye Falls while he was employed on Ralph Warren's farm just east of the village. On Monday afternoon, August 2, 1917, Frank was in Warren's barn preparing to take a load of hay to the village. He saw Warren's young son with a gun.

Warren's son was only seven years old. He had taken his father's shotgun loaded with No. 6 birdshot to scare the crows in the cornfield. Farmers' children learned early in life how to handle guns—especially for scaring crows.

When Frank Potter came upon the boy with the gun, he asked him what he intended to do with it. The boy replied, "Hunting Germans." It was 1917, and we were engaged in a war, so Frank did not give the boy a second thought. He proceeded to load the wagon and hitch the horse. A little while later, as he was passing a high board fence that went around the barnyard, the gun went off. The charge grazed the back of Potter's head, which appeared just above the top of the fence.

The recoil from the shotgun knocked down the seven-year-old. When he got up, he ran to the house to tell his father. "I shot a German," he said. His father ran out and found Potter bleeding freely. Luckily, Dr. Marlatte, the local doctor, was driving by and witnessed the accident. He quickly rendered first aid and took Mr. Potter home.

The boy never realized what he had done. Mr. Potter recovered from his wounds. The United States won World War I, making the world "safe for democracy."

Bibliography

Honeoye Falls' Good Name Tainted

Document from Western House of Refuge, August 11, 1849.
Rochester (NY) Democrat & Chronicle. "Century Old State School..." October 2, 1849.

"I'm a Dead Man"

Ancestry.com. James Lorance Williams Family Tree. 2009.
Attica (NY) Morning Herald. Untitled article. December 17, 1858.
Batavia (NY) Daily Morning News. "Death of a Noted Criminal." October 21, 1879.
Buffalo (NY) Currier. "Coroners' Cases." October 20, 1879.
Census Records for Mendon (New York State and federal). 1850, 1855, 1860, 1865, 1870, 1875, 1880.
Ellicottville (NY) Republican. "General Jail Delivery." December 13, 1857.
Examiner.com. "The Strange Defense of Manley Locke." June 19, 2012.
Genesee County (NY) Herald. Untitled article. January 8, 1858.
New York Times. "Another Murder Trial at Rochester." October 19, 1858.
Rochester Union and Advertiser. "Benjamin Starr Account of Inquest." November 2, 1857

———. "Benjamin Starr Killed By Manley Locke." October 30, 1857.

———. "Court of Oyer and Terminer." October 11, 1858.

———. "Departure of Locke." January 5, 1859.

———. "Honeoye Falls Citizens Held Meeting to Discuss Murder." November 6, 1857.

———. "Manley Locke Again." March 17, 1876.

———. "Manley Locke Dead." October 2, 1879.

———. "The Murder at Honeoye Falls." November 7, 1857.

INSANITY KILLS AGAIN

Burial Records. Honeoye Falls (New York) Cemetery.

Census Records for Mendon (New York State and federal). 1850, 1855, 1860.

Genesee Weekly Democrat. "Another Murder in Honeoye Falls." June 5, 1858.

Geneva (NY) Courier. "Woman Shot Dead by her Husband." June 9, 1858.

Geneva (NY) Gazette. "Yacente DuPlante." June 9, 1858.

Monroe County (New York) Insane Asylum Admission Ledger. 1866.*Rochester Democrat & American.* "Another Murder at Honeoye Falls." June 1, 1858.

———. "Commitment of DuPlante." June 5, 1858.

———. "Contradiction." June 2, 1858.

———. "Court Record." June 29, 1858.

Rochester Union and Advertiser. "DuPlante Returned to Rochester Insane Asylum." December 16, 1866.

———. "DuPlante Yacente Deliberately Shot Wife." October 11, 1858.

———. "Yacente DuPlante Held for Shooting Wife." May 31, 1858.

———. "Yacente DuPlante Indicted for Murder." June 29, 1858.

———. "Yacente DuPlante Probability of Discharge." February 11, 1867.

———. "Yacente DuPlante Refused to Escape." December 13, 1858.

Utica (New York) Insane Asylum. Federal Census for 1860.

BURGLARY OF THE POST OFFICE

Census Records (New York State and federal). 1850, 1855, 1860, 1865, 1870.
1872 Map of Honeoye Falls.

Rochester Union and Advertiser. "Arrest of Spellacy." March 23, 1858.

————. "Honeoye Falls Post Office Robbers." January 22, 1859.

————. "NY Soldiers Arrived in Washington." May 22, 1862.

————. "Post Office Robbery." January 21, 1859.

————. "Sentenced to Auburn." May 24, 1859.

U.S. Civil War Soldiers' Records.

ANOTHER STARR MURDERED

Oswego (NY) Commercial Times. "At Rochester, James Murphy on Trial." February 12, 1864.

Rochester Democrat & American. "Murder Trial 4th Day." February 12, 1864.

————. "Names of Jurors Chosen," February 9, 1864

Rochester Union & Advertiser. "Honeoye Falls Homicide." July 24, 1863.

————. "James Murphy Arrested for Murder." July 23, 1863.

————. "James Murphy Convicted of Murder." February 12, 1864.

————. "James Murphy: Names of Jurors Chosen." February 9, 1864.

————. "James Murphy on Trial for Murder." February 8, 1864.

————. "James Murphy Proceedings of 3rd Day Trial." February 10, 1864.

————. "James Murphy Sentenced to 10 Years and 3 Months." February 14, 1864.

————. "James Murphy to Go on Trial." January 13, 1864.

————. "The Murphy Trial." February 11, 1864.

————. "Prisoner Arraigned." October 14, 1863.

————. "Sentence of Murphy." February 15, 1864.

MURDER OR SELF-DEFENSE?

Monroe County (New York) Almshouse Records.

Rochester Daily Democrat. "Honeoye Falls Homicide." November 19, 1869.

Rochester Orphan Asylum Record of Indentures.

Rochester Union and Advertiser. "John & Catherine Donlon on Trial." February 17, 1870.

————. "John & Catherine Donlon Proceedings of Trial." February 18, 1870.

———. "John Donlon Found Not Guilty of First Degree." January 8, 1870.

———. "John Donlon Sentenced to Auburn Prison." February 19, 1870.

———. "John Donnelly and Wife Held for Criminal Assault." November 16, 1869.

———. "List of Murderers in County Jail." February 21, 1870.

———. "Murderer Taken to Sing Sing." February 26, 1870.

———. "Trial of John & Catherine Donlon." February 15, 1870.

———. "Wm. Gates Murdered by Mr. & Mrs. John Donnelly." November 19, 1869.

MURDER AT THE JUNCTION

Buffalo Express. "Spencer Howe Murdered with Stiletto." March 26, 1894.

Honeoye Falls Post Express. "DeNardo Acquitted." June 14, 1894.

———. "The DeNardo Trial." June 13, 1894.

———. "Hard to Identify." June 12, 1894.

———. "An Italian's Knife." March 26, 1894.

———. "The Italian's Version." March 3, 1894.

Rochester Democrat & Chronicle. "DeNardo Is Caught." April 2, 1894.

———. "DeNardo's Trial in Jury's Hands." June 14, 1894.

———. "For Defending DeNardo." July 13, 1894.

———. "Have a Story to Tell." May 12, 1894.

———. "Hunting the Murderer." March 27, 1894.

———. "No Word of Defense." June 13, 1894.

———. "Struck Down by a Dago." March 26, 1894.

Rochester Union and Advertiser. "Horrible Murder." March 26, 1894.

———. "Nicolo DeNardo Accused of Murder." March 27, 1894.

———. "Nicolo DeNardo Captured." April 2, 1894.

———. "Nicolo DeNardo on Trial for Murder." June 11, 1894.

———. "Nicolo DeNardo Pleaded Not Guilty." May 29, 1894.

———. "Nicolo DeNardo Trial for Murder to Begin." June 6, 1894.

———. "Spencer Howe Three Suspected in Murder." March 28, 1894.

MONEY MAYHEM

Rochester Democrat & Chronicle. "Argument Brings About Shooting." June 2, 1914.
———. "Bad Money at Honeoye Falls." September 2, 1903.
———. "Honeoye Falls Bad Money Men Guilty." November 12, 1903.
———. "Old House at Honeoye Falls Yields Up More Spurious Coins." September 3, 1903.
———. "Scholl's Story of the Capture." September 4, 1903.
———. "Sentence of Counterfeiters." November 14, 1903.
———. "Waived Examination." September 6, 1903.
———. "Whitbeck a Victim." May 10, 1900.

MISSES DOG—KILLS WIFE

Census Records for Mendon (federal). 1900, 1910, 1920, 1930, 1940.
Groveland (New York) Correctional Center Census. 1910, 1915.
Honeoye Falls Times. "Fatal Shooting Accident." September 8, 1909.
Pittsford (New York) Cemetery Records.
Rochester Democrat & Chronicle. "Accidental Killing Is Coroner's Finding." September 19, 1909.
———. "All Not Clear to Officials." August 30, 1909.
———. "Bail Put up for Kirschner." September 23, 1909.
———. "Grand Jury Makes Report." October 16, 1909.
———. "Mendon Center Man Shoots Wife." September 4, 1909.
———. "Mendon Farmer Held for Shooting." August 29, 1909.
———. "No One Saw Farmhand Fire Shot." September 3, 1909.

LOVE-LOST MURDER

Honeoye Falls Times. "Italian Shooting Affair." September 8, 1910.
———. "Mrs. Ralph Roberts (Mellie Stefano) Dies." October 6, 1966.
———. "The Stefano Shooting Affair." September 15, 1910.
———. "Suitor Died of His Self-Inflicted Wounds." February 1, 1911.
Rochester Democrat & Chronicle. "Jilted Suitor Shoots Girl in Her Home." September 9, 1910.

Rochester Union and Advertiser. "His Condition Serious." September 13, 1910.
———. "Italian Conscious." September 11, 1910.
———. "Jealous Italian Shoots Girl Three Times." September 9, 1910.
———. "Man Dying & Girl in Critical Condition." September 10, 1910.
———. "Would-Be Murderer Regains His Senses." N.d.
———. "Youthful Italian in Dying Condition." N.d.

ONTARIO STREET MURDER

Auburn Prison (New York) Electrocution Registry. 1870–1916.
Honeoye Falls Times. "Brutal Assault & Murder of James Duffy." February 23, 1911.
Rochester Democrat & Chronicle. "Death May Save Him from Electrocution." August 13, 1911.
———. "People Rest in Williams' Murder Case." June 2, 1911.
———. "Three Witnesses' Evidence Strongly." June 1, 1911.
Rochester Union and Advertiser. "Irresponsibility Plea for Williams Seriously Shaken." June 2, 1911.
———. "Negro Tries Suicide When Found Guilty." June 4, 1911.
———. "Slayer of James Duffy on Trial for Murder." June 1, 1911.
———. "Williams Convicted as Indicted." June 5, 1911.

DEAD UNDER THE TREE

Honeoye Falls Times. "Farm Hand Thought to Have Been Murdered." July 18, 1912.
Rochester Democrat & Chronicle. "Manslaughter Hearing Over." September 12, 1912.
———. "May Be Evidence of Foul Play." July 13, 1912.
———. "No Indictments." October 11, 1912.
Rochester Union and Advertiser. "Rochester Man Died after Day Haying." July 12, 1912.
———. "Two Held for Manslaughter Following Death." July 13, 1912.

"I Thought She Was Dead"

Leader Republican (Gloversville, NY). "Rochester Beating Case Unsolved." February 29, 1944.

Niagara Falls (NY) Gazette. "Hold Youths in Gonzalez Robbery." March 3, 1944.

Rochester Democrat & Chronicle. "Guilt Denied by Two Youths in Kidnapping." March 15, 1944.

———. "Police Solve Dual Custody." March 3, 1944.

———. "Two Indicted in Gonzalez Kidnap Case." March 14, 1944.

———. "Youths Get Long Terms for Attack." April 23, 1944.

Junkyard Murder

Canandaigua (NY) Messenger. "December Slaying." June 8, 1973.

Citizen Advertiser (Auburn, NY). "Body Found." December 28, 1972.

Front Page Detective magazine. "Murder in the Lair of the Wolfman." January 16, 1973.

Geneva (NY) Times. "Ontario County Man Charged with Murder." December 30, 1972.

———. "Youth Pleads Guilty to Manslaughter." January 17, 1973.

Honeoye Falls Times. "They're Cleaning Up the Junk." N.d.

Interview with Emily Manzler, ret. detective (photos).

Interview with Harry DeHollander, ret. Sergeant.

Rochester Democrat & Chronicle. "Ex-Employee Charged in Murder of Junkman." December 30, 1972.

———. "Police Call It Murder." December 29, 1972.

———. "Recluse Found Slain," December 28, 1972.

———. "Recluse's Epitaph a Pile of Trash." December 29, 1972.

———. "Routine Call for Repairman." December 29, 1972.

———. "Slain Recluse's Junkyard Hasn't Been Touched Yet." January 8, 1973.

Rochester Times-Union. "Complaints Grow with Junk." June 12, 1972.

———. "Old Auto Yields Clues to Slaying." December 29, 1972.

———. "Youth Indicted in Recluse Slaying." February 10, 1973.

Railroad Mayhem

The New York Central Railroad

Honeoye Falls Cemetery Records.
Honeoye Falls Times. "A Damage Suit Probable." November 10, 1904.
———. "Lorin Parsons Killed on Main Street Crossing." September 1, 1904.
Monroe County Mail. "Death of Loren G. Parsons." September 1, 1904.

The Lehigh Valley Railroad

Honeoye Falls Times. "Father Cluney Narrowly Escapes Death." February 3, 1916.

Miscellaneous Mayhem

Disaster in a Hand Basket

Utica Daily Press. "Blown to Pieces with Dynamite." July 25, 1912.

"Hunting Germans"

Honeoye Falls Times. Untitled article. August 5, 1917.

About the Authors

Diane Ham was born in Oklahoma, grew up in Michigan, spent a few years in Kentucky and has lived in the Rochester, New York area for forty-four years. She has a BS degree in business administration from Central Michigan University. She has been town historian in Mendon, where she currently lives, for thirty-five years. She has written several books and booklets on Mendon subjects. She became a registered historian of New York State in 2005 and is also president of the Monroe County Municipal Historians and a member of the Association of Public Historians of New York State. In her spare time, she and her husband of fifty years enjoy renovating their old farmhouse, camping and traveling. They have two married sons and two granddaughters.

Lynne Menz was born in Hanover, New Hampshire, and is a retired middle school social studies teacher and former Social Studies Department chairperson. She has a BS degree in social studies education from the State University of New York at Albany. She and her husband live in a Greek Revival house that has been in the Menz family for nearly one hundred years. She is currently the Honeoye Falls, New York village historian (Town of Mendon) and secretary of the local historical society. This book was born out of a program for the historical society on train wrecks and tragedies in Honeoye Falls and Mendon. Lynne and her husband enjoy traveling all over the world. They have one married daughter and one granddaughter. She and Diane are both members of the Mendon Bicentennial Committee for the Town of Mendon's Bicentennial—2013.

Visit us at
www.historypress.net
··
This title is also available as an e-book